Beth,

Good luck !

(908) 429-0192

# DIAMONDS:

## *Know What You Are Buying & Selling*

*By*

### B.J. Tadena
**Master Diamond Cutter**

**Rough Stones Co., Inc.**
**New York, NY**

ISBN  0-9675148-0-0

Library of Congress Cataloguing -In-Publication Data

**Diamonds :** *Know What You Are Buying & Selling*
All rights reserved.

Copyright © 1999 by *B.J. Tadena*

Printed by Bookcrafters, Fredericksburg, VA
Printed in the U.S.A.

*Cover Design by Nuby G. De Leon*

*The author wishes to thank
M.Cristina F. Bada and Lorna E. Luz
for their enormous help
in the completion of this book.*

i

## *This One Is For You*

*T*o my late parents, Benjamin, Sr. and Priscilla Tadena, as well as to my lovely sisters for their kind support and patience all this time; to my wonderful family whose faith in me inspired and encouraged me to write this book; and to the Lord Almighty who has guided me and changed my life through His Word in *"Power For Living"*, this one is for you .

I love you all.

B.J. Tadena

# Preface

In a book published in 77 A.D., the Roman historian C. Plinius Secundus thus said "...to tell you the truth, there is no fraud or deceit in the world which yields greater gain and profit than that of counterfeiting gems." Then as now, because of the value that man has given to gemstones, there is always the persistent lure to replicate them. Much more so for diamonds. Because of its rarity, beauty, durability, portability and tradition, the demand for diamonds is high. Following the fundamental principle of economics, a commodity that possesses these characteristics will naturally have high commercial worth. This book is written with the end in view of enhancing the awareness of the ordinary buyers and owners of diamonds, for them to know more about these assets. Knowing about diamonds before one buys or sells them obviates the possibility for the consumer to fall victim to fraud. Of course, one should also know about simulants --- how they differentiate from natural diamonds. Be aware of the characteristics. It is also my desire to share my many, many years of experience as a diamond cutter who knows the intrinsic qualities of the diamond --- its guts and innards, so to speak. I have known diamonds, have created their many facets and shaped the precise angles that have given these cold stones their life, essence and fire. Nothing can perfectly replicate a diamond because nothing can perfectly replicate nature. The diamond --- a gift of nature, the teardrop of the good earth.

**B.J. Tadena**

# Table of Contents

Chapter                                                        Page

.................................................... **Part I**

| 1 | Mystical, Magical Madness | 5 |
| 2 | Birth Of A Diamond | 17 |
| 3 | Anatomy Of A Gemstone Diamond | 27 |
| 4 | The Art Of Cutting The Diamond | 31 |

.................................................... **Part II**

| 5 | Instruments For Evaluation And Grading | 51 |
| 6 | Cut | 59 |
| 7 | Clarity | 69 |
| 8 | Color | 83 |
| 9 | Carat | 91 |

.................................................... **Part III**

| 10 | Simulants And Synthetic Diamonds | 101 |
| 11 | Investing On Diamonds For Profit And Pleasure | 109 |
| 12 | Consumer Tips | 113 |

**APPENDIX**

| ◆ Diamond Consumer's Bill of Rights | 116 |
| ◆ Price Guide | 120 |
| ◆ Internationally Recognized Laboratories For Certification Reports on Authenticity and Quality | 141 |
| ◆ Directory of Gemological Laboratories in the United States | 142 |
| ◆ International Directory of Gemological Associations | 187 |
| ◆ International Directory of Gemological Laboratories | 197 |
| ◆ Diamond Price Sources | 207 |
| ◆ Tools and Equipments Suppliers | 208 |

**BIBLIOGRAPHY**

**ABOUT THE AUTHOR**

1

# Part I

*Twinkling....*

*Sparkling...*

*Splendor...*

*The Diamond*

# 1

## *Mystical, Magical Madness*

*D*iamonds! The mere thought of these magnificent stones brings to mind a dazzling spectacle of prismatic colors. The word itself rouses the imagination to the glitter, the glamour and the grandeur of gems sparkling in splendor and luminous lucidity. We have seen diamonds as expensive gems set in ornate jewelry. They are imposing and brilliant stones enthroned in gold or silver casting giving its wearer the air of affluence, success and power. We have seen the diamond as a gem but very few of us have seen the rough stone from whence come not just the gem but the industrial diamond as well.

The diamonds that we now encounter were formed millions of years ago in a fiery furnace deep into the earth. Intense heat and extreme pressure transform pure carbon into diamonds. But unlike other carbon-based minerals, the diamond has a crystalline structure owing to the three dimensional pattern into which its atomic particles are arranged. This kind of pattern forms a cube, which gives the diamond its extraordinary strength and, thus, proved as the hardest natural substance known. Forced out of the earth's depth through volcanic eruptions, diamonds are brought to the earth's surface by the flowing magma. When the volcanic activity subsides and cooling takes place, the diamonds remain immured in solid magma known as "blue ground" or kimberlite.

As the diamond gem is to jewelry, the diamond used for industrial purposes is called the bort. It is the diamond that is poorly crystallized or of inferior color and fragmented. These are used as abrasives in the cutting of diamonds or used as cutting heads of rock drills, sawing blades and glasscutters. Other uses are as diamond scribers, engravers, phonograph needles and miniature carbide tooling, etc. From the Greek words *adamas*, meaning unconquerable and *diaphanes*, meaning transparent, diamonds were first discovered in India in 800 B.C. From then until the early part of the 18th century, India was the sole producer of diamonds. In the first quarter of the 18th century, diamonds were also discovered in Brazil. Sources say that Brazilian diamonds may have been discovered much earlier but were referred to as *"carbonados"*.

In 1867, the first major diamond discovery in South Africa was made by a child who found a beautiful pebble on the banks of the Orange River, 500 miles north of Capetown. He took this home and played with it like a toy. It was a diamond weighing 21.25 carats. Two years later, an influx of prospectors and miners rushed in when a bushman found an even finer stone in the same area. He swapped this for 500 sheep, 10 oxen and a horse. This was quite an expensive trade in those times but the man who made the trade in turn sold the stone, a superb 84 carat white diamond, for $50,000 to the British Colonial Secretary in Capetown. This diamond, later called *"The Star of Africa"* was cut and polished into a pear-shaped diamond for the Countess of Dudley.

The rush of prospectors, who were enticed by the thought of diamonds glittering in the sun, gave rise to the shantytown which they called Kimberley, after the British Colonial Secretary of the time. Some of the diamond hunters were lucky enough to strike it rich because the diamonds were relatively easy to find lying in unique plots of yellowish clay. When the diamonds on the surface were exhausted, dry diggings started and more diamonds were found underneath in a layer of "blue ground" or kimberlite. More of this will be discussed in the next chapter.

### The Hope Diamond

Back in the 17th century, stories about India's exotic wealth reached Europe. In 1642, French trader and diamond collector, Jean Baptiste Travernier bought a striking and rare blue diamond with a reputed 200-year history behind it. The diamond weighed at 112.5 carats and was mined from the Kistna River in southwest India. Before Travernier bought the blue diamond, a Hindu priest once had possession of it having stolen this from the forehead of an Indian temple idol. The priest was caught and put to death by torture. Apparently, he was the first victim of the curse of the blue diamond. Travernier sold the blue diamond but was later torn to death by a pack of wild dogs. The gem reappeared in the possession of King Louis XIV who had it cut to 67.5 carats. He soon died a broken man who was so much hated by his people. His highly vaunted Empire crumbled after a series of military catastrophes. Legend has it that after this, Louis XIV's eldest son, his eldest grandson and his great-grandson fell victims to the curse within a year. The diamond vanished in 1792 and resurfaced again in 1832, this time as a gift of the Russian Prince Ivan Kanitovski to his Parisian mistress whom he shot dead. He himself was murdered afterwards. The next place the blue diamond surfaced was in Amsterdam where a jeweler named Fals sheared it to its present weight of 44.5 carats. The new size did not seem to affect the curse. Fals died poor and his son, who stole the diamond from him, committed suicide out of guilt.

The jewel continued to be passed on from hand to bloody hand across Europe --- and, in 1830, to Henry Thomas Hope, a very wealthy London Banker, who bought it for $150,000 and gave the blue diamond its name. The curse spared him, but not his grandson who inherited the diamond. His marriage broke and he died penniless. The Hope diamond next appeared in Russia when it was acquired by Catherine the Great. She had a tumultuous life and died of apoplexy all of a sudden. In 1908, a Turkish merchant sold the Hope diamond to Turkish Sultan Abdul Hamid who bought it for his wife for $400,000. Shortly after, the merchant and his family all died in a vehicular accident. The Sultan, on the other hand, presented the gift to his wife, Subaya, then stabbed her. He lost his throne a year later.

The 44.5 carat *Hope Diamond* is on permanent loan by Harry Winston to the National Museum of Natural History, Smithsonian Institution, Washington, DC.

It was while honeymooning in Turkey also in 1908 that Edward McLean, heir to the *Washington Post*, and his wife Evalyn first saw the Hope diamond on the neck of the sultan's favorite wife. For months and years after they had already returned to Washington, D.C., Evalyn could not put the fiery blue diamond off her mind. Like a mesmerizing dream, she was totally seduced by its beauty. It was as if its ice-cold heart was calling out to her. When she later heard that the sultan had been deposed, she quickly arranged to buy the stone notwithstanding its renowned reputation. Pierre Cartier bought the stone in France and sold it to Evalyn for $154,000. Over the next 40 years after acquiring the Hope diamond, Edward McLean's mother

Evalyn Walsh McLean wears the *Hope Diamond.*

died; his nine-year old son was run down by a car and died; McLean was financially ruined and died in a mental institution; his daughter died of drug overdose and his wife Evalyn fell, broke her hip, became a morphine addict and contracted yet another illness from which she never survived. A year after the death of Evalyn Walsh McLean, jeweler Harry Winston of New York bought the blue stone from the heirs of the McLean family. He escaped the hex of the infamous Hope diamond. He placed this on "permanent loan" to the Smithsonian Institute in Washington, D.C.

### *The Koh-i-noor*

This famous diamond was first owned by the Raja of Malwa in India in 1304. It was part of the treasure of the Mogul Emperors for 400 years until the Nadir Shah of Persia (now Iran) invaded India in 1739 and took the diamond. In 1747 however, a palace revolt took place, the Nadir Shah was killed, and his relatives squabbled over the Koh-i-noor. A hundred years later, the Koh-i-noor was the brightest jewel in the turban of the Sikh Empire when its male-dominated lands were taken over by the British colonizers. The East India Company seized the Koh-i-noor and presented the stone to Queen Victoria in 1850. The Koh-i-noor, which means *"mountain of light"*, originally weighed 186.5 carats but Queen Victoria was still not too happy with its lack of luster and had it recut to 108.93 carats. When she did this, the Koh-i-noor further scintillated, sparkled and became more aglow with fire. It is now still part of the British royal treasure.

The *Koh-i-noor* "Mountain of Light." The present Queen Mother's crown is at the Tower of London. On the lower cross is the *Koh-i-noor*.

11

There are two myths behind the Koh-i-noor: that its owner will rule the world and that it must never be worn by a man. This stone has sparked destruction and devastation in its trail when it was in the possession of male rulers and yet, it has glittered since then over the heads of three Queens of England. No British King has ever worn it. It now reposes in the Tower of London, encased in the crown of Queen Elizabeth, the Queen Mother.

### The Orloff

The Orloff was known to be the eye of the statue of Brahma in Mysore (India) at the start of the 18th century. Risking life and limb, a French soldier pried it out and stole it in 1750. He then sold this to the captain of an English ship for $10,000. In London, a dealer bought it from the captain for $60,000 and was in turn sold to Prince Orloff of Russia for $450,000 in 1773. The diamond since then was called the Orloff and has remained a part of the imperial treasury, now a state collection, of Russia.

### The Cullinan

The largest piece of diamond ever mined is the Cullinan, named after its finder, Thomas Cullinan. Discovered in 1905 at Pretoria, South Africa, the Cullinan weighed at 3,106 carats. It was bought by the

Transvaal government in 1907 for £150,000 and was presented to King Edward VII on his 60th birthday.

The rough stone *Cullinan* diamond, the largest piece of diamond ever mined weighing at 3,106 carats. This diamond was later cut into 105 separate diamond gems, the largest of which is the *Star of Africa* mounted in the royal scepter of England.

On February 10, 1908 in Amsterdam, expert diamond cutter and the world's most experienced in his time, Jacob Asscher, was faced with the intricate and stressful job of cutting the Cullinan which was nearly 1½ pounds in weight and about 5 inches across. Asscher laid a cleaver along a groove in the stone that he meticulously plotted. The smallest error that he makes in cutting the stone will leave him with just a pile of diamond shreds. He made his first attempt and tapped down a heavy steel rod. The tool blade snapped. He asked for another tool blade and proceeded to try again. The blade worked on his next blow and the stone was cut. Asscher Jacob fainted and when he regained consciousness, he had two pieces of high-priced stones, which he cut into 105 separate diamond gems. The largest among them, the Cullinan I, was 530.20 carats and known as the *Great Star of Africa*. Pear-shaped, it was mounted in the Royal Scepter of England. The second largest was set in the Imperial State Crown and the rest all became part of the royal jewels of the British Royal Family kept in the Tower of London.

The *Star of Africa*

As the adventurer and diamond collector/trader Jean Baptiste Travernier once wrote, "A gem without a history is more than just a passing interest." Because of its rarity and extreme beauty, the diamond has held itself in magnificence over all other gemstones. The Greeks of old believed that the fiery brilliance in a diamond symbolized the flame and represented the passion of love. They also wore a diamond in battle as a symbol of courage and bravery. The people of ancient India, on the other hand, believed that diamonds had the power to make them invincible. They also believed that it can cure one of impotence and madness. In some parts of Asia, it is still believed that wearing a diamond is a protection from witchcraft and sorcery. Yet amidst all these beliefs, ancient or presenttime, it is the financial logic that is credible above all. Having a good quality diamond or two is a handy asset that can certainly tide you over a life-breaking, nerve-wrecking crisis, financial or otherwise. For today, the diamond is not just a thing of beauty, it is a very portative safety net.

# 2

*Birth Of A Diamond*

There is a quaint and unusual way that the good earth shares with us her bounties. In the case of diamonds that form deep within the earth, these marvelous stones are able to reach the surface only through volcanic eruptions. But this is just nature's transport. How a diamond is formed is a wonder by itself --- a natural phenomenon that modern laboratories have long tried and are still trying to replicate.

A hundred miles or so deep into the earth is a natural laboratory where diamonds are assiduously and patiently being formed. The conditions are constant. Excessive pressure and extreme heat for no less than 2 billion years created the diamonds that are now being used as highly valuable gems or parts of some of the most powerful industrial tools and high tech machinery. A diamond is made of pure carbon in crystalline form. Volcanic eruptions make it possible for diamonds to reach the earth's surface and it takes another yet "perfect condition" for a diamond to remain as a diamond. This "perfect condition" is nature's way of preparing the diamond properly. When the erupting volcano emits molten rocks, called magma, onto the earth's surface, the potential diamond should not be buried too deep into the molten rock, otherwise the diamond will seethe and go back to being a free carbon atom set to fuse with other elements to create an altogether different compound. If, upon reaching the earth's surface, the cooling process is slow, the potential diamond will turn into graphite, that dark, carbon-based mineral used as pencil lead, electrodes, lubricants and crucibles. And, should the potential diamond, upon reaching the earth's crust, connect with oxygen while it is still hot, it will evaporate as carbon dioxide. A potential diamond will remain and survive as a diamond only if it is quickly cooled upon reaching the earth's surface. Then its formation is completed as a properly prepared rough diamond ready to last for years and years.

During the process of volcanic eruption, the diamond-bearing magma rises to the surface and is blasted out through volcanic craters and fissures. When the volcanic activity subsides and cooling takes place, the diamonds are left imbedded in igneous rocks or solidified magma called kimberlite or "blue ground". As time passes and erosion takes place, some of the surface diamonds, either still imbedded in volcanic rocks or have been exposed by the action of wind and rain, are eroded and carried by storms, water currents, glaciers, sleet or melted snow, towards river banks and lake shores usually a considerable distance from where the kimberlite pipes spewed them out. Because of this, diamonds are mined from two sources --- from kimberlite pipes or from alluvial deposits. Later, explorers and geologists discovered that lamproites also produce diamonds.

Kimberlites are narrow, pipelike fissures and carrot-shaped funnels that are serpentinized deep into the ground. They contain a variety of minerals, including diamonds, and are therefore considered as the principal conveyor of diamonds. But not all kimberlite pipes contain diamonds. Only about 10 percent of all known kimberleys are diamondiferous and less than two percent have commercial amounts of diamonds.

1. Volcanic eruption occurs and magma spews from under the earth.

2. Volcanic activity subsides.

3. Magma cools and solidifies as kimberlite pipes about 100 miles below earth's crust.

4. Kimberlite pipes or "blue ground" encase diamonds and other mineral deposits.

The number of rough diamonds that have been mined all over the world has so far reached the total of 110 million carats. Of this, only less than 50 percent qualify as gems and the rest are for industrial use. Before the discovery of other diamond mines, India held the prestige and honor of having first discovered diamonds and, from its bounteous alluvial deposits, produced, for centuries, the finest and most celebrated diamonds in history. Golconda, India was the greatest diamond center of the ancient world. But just when the supply of diamonds in India declined, diamonds were discovered in the mid-18th century in Brazil. For awhile, Brazil became the major supplier of diamonds until the discovery of the enormous diamond sources in South Africa in 1867 which still continue to produce rough diamonds until now. Later explorations and discoveries have unearthed diamonds also in other parts of the African continent like Botswana, Sierra Leone, Guinea as well as in Australia and Russia. Notwithstanding these discoveries, the diamond has remained the peerless "King of Gems" --- rare, fascinating, adamantine, valuable ... and expensive.

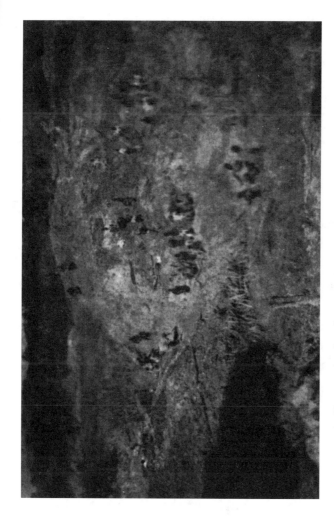

A diamond mine in Conakry, Republic of Guinea.

## *Industrial Diamonds and Synthetic Diamonds*

The advent of industrialization, scientific breakthroughs and modern technology uncovered the functional capability of the diamond. The diamonds of lower quality, those that cannot pass for gems and are called bort, are used for industrial purposes because of their characteristic hardness and a considerably higher tolerance for heat and pressure. Where other materials such as steel, tungsten carbide, iron, granite, marble, glass or other fabricated constituents break, wear out or become dull, the diamond tool is still operative and serviceable. As an abrasive, the pulverized diamond coated on grinding machines can do the job more efficiently and effectively than any other abrasive. The diamond indeed responds well to the extreme requirements of various industries in the use of materials. It is afterall the hardest natural substance. Useful as it is, however, the availability of the industrial diamond is one factor that consumers had to contend with.

The synthetic diamond was invented a few years after World War II when United States, like the other nations all over the world, was faced with the necessity of rebuilding after the chaos and destruction of war. Somehow, the appalling realization was that there was not enough supply of the natural diamonds to provide for the needs of the various industries. And because the supply was not enough, using these for wide scale application was not possible.

Enter General Electric. By replicating the underground conditions of tremendous heat and extreme pressure, General Electric was able to create, in their laboratory, the synthetic diamond out of carbon. The new invention served the needs of industries as well as the natural industrial diamonds could. There was a marked increase in the demand for synthetic diamonds to be used for grinding, sawing, cutting and as polishing agents especially in manufacturing. Although producing the synthetic diamonds was costly at that time, there was a market for them and, therefore, the return of investments was assured. Eventually, De Beers, the company that has worldwide monopoly over the distribution, allocation and marketing of natural diamonds, also joined in the production of synthetic diamonds for industrial use. Today, other countries have joined the United States in manufacturing synthetic industrial diamonds: Russia, Japan, China, India, Holland, Finland, South Africa, Sweden and Ireland (the industries in the last three countries mentioned are related to the De Beers group).

The use of synthetic diamonds has further expanded, thanks to the creative imagination and inquisitive thinking of our modern scientists and design engineers. Synthetic diamonds can be manufactured for a wider functional purpose. In the automotive industry, industrial diamonds are used to make engine blocks and pistons. Because these are made from very abrasive high silica aluminum, diamond cutting tools are preferred because they withstand heat and do not wear out as easily as other conventional materials. The use of diamond cutting tools increases tool life 50 to 100 times longer. Bort, as industrial diamonds are called, is used in cleaving tools to cut through glass for the fiber optics industry. For the plastics industry, bort is used if plastics manufacturers desire mirror finishes on their acrylic pieces. In electronics, microscopic diamond cubes are incorporated in communications satellites to keep transistors cool. There are a lot of other uses of bort in industries. It is used in the fabrication of sensors that are sensitive to heat or light, such that a diamond-coated glass allows the light rays to go through unbended or provides a safe barrier between the heat-sensitive sensor and the user. Diamond-tipped surgical blades and scalpels can be used more times than conventional stainless steel that do not retain its sharpness after a couple of uses.

The manufacture of synthetic diamonds is again something borne out of necessity. Synthetic diamonds are being used in ways that a lot of us do not know because we are seldom afforded the opportunity to see them or to know that they are there. Manufacturing industries, the military, aeronautics, and the various medical fields have benefited a great deal out of the invention of synthetic diamonds. Without doubt, a material as tough as the diamond, which is even harder than steel or granite, certainly has numerous uses for man other than adorning his body and a symbol of his status. Yet, the diamond is better known for its aristocratic beauty than for being a workman's tool of trade.

On the other hand, simulants, the synthetic diamonds that are manufactured, cut and shaped like diamond gems, are the resultant effort of some gem dealers to come up with a cheaper alternative to natural diamonds. Honest dealers disclose that these are simulants and are either cubic zirconia, Russian diamonds or moissanites. But other dealers might not give the same truthful disclosure and could pass them to their customers as natural diamonds. This is where it hurts because the temptation to profit a hundredfold lurks behind the deal that involves a simulant being passed off as a diamond. Needless to say that most buyers of diamonds make their purchases by virtue of trust --- trusting the credibility and honesty of the dealer. It is in buying diamonds that trust is established. Yet, it is also in buying diamonds that trust can be broken. Other merchandise can be easily inspected and examined prior to purchase. The diamond is one commodity that you must know and know fully well before acquiring because, then, you may be paying for just the illusion, not the reality, a whiff but not the breath of the peerless "King of Gems".

# 3 *Anatomy Of The Gemstone Diamond*

Knowing the gemstone diamond means being familiar with the parts of the gem. As complicated and intricate a diamond may be, its glitter and scintillation comes from the detailed execution of its parts. This gift of nature, having been enhanced by man through his skill in the creation of angles and planes on the stone, now treats the beholder to a wondrous display of sublime beauty, of silent yet grandiose magnificence, of fire in ice. Being informed of how the play of light is intricately accomplished bolsters one's appreciation of the stone even more.

The polished diamond is made up of its structural components. These components, or parts, are present in every diamond regardless of its shape and size. The components are the crown, the girdle and the pavilion.

The parts of the diamond are made up of various facets. *Facets* are the polished plane surfaces that are seen on a gem. The position and relative angle of each facet to one another cause the brilliancy and fire in the stone. It is in the positioning of the facets that the play of lights is achieved creating, in turn, the enchanting display of prismatic colors. It is the light dispersion within the stone bouncing off at angles that makes fire possible. This phenomenon is not possible for all gems.

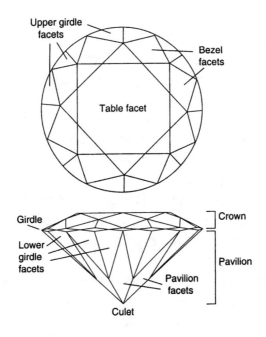

Components of a *diamond* including *facets*

The top part of the diamond is called the *crown*. At its center is a large facet called the table. The *girdle* is the thin area, or the rim, that separates the top part (crown) from the bottom portion, called the *pa-*

*vilion.* The facets that comprise the area from the table to the girdle are called the star facet, the upper bezel facet and the upper girdle facet.

The *pavilion* ends with the culet, which is the facet at the bottom tip of the diamond. The facets that extend from the culet to the girdle are known as the lower girdle facets and the pavilion facets or lower bezel facets.

Since we have opted in this book to start from the basics, at this point it might as well be discussed why the universal symbol for diamond is this shape ♦ (as in the ace of diamonds). This is because the common shape of the rough diamond is octahedron. The octahedron is a non-perfect form of the cubic system. It is a figure with eight sides built in such a way that when sawed in half, two pyramids, each with four sides, is created. With each pyramid, a diamond cutter can make a round brilliant cut, its apex becoming the culet and the flat bottom becoming the top of the diamond.

When buying a diamond, having your own rough diamond to be cut according to your specified shape or desiring to have your old miners recut, it is to your advantage if you know the parts of the diamond. Suffice it to say that it is easier to communicate with the jeweler, dealer or diamond cutter if you know the

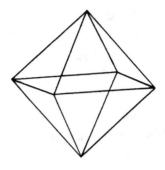

*Octahedron Diamond Crystal*

terminology. It is your diamond after all --- your investment, your pleasure.

# 4 *The Art of Cutting the Diamond*

Although its rarity and strength are the primary reasons for the diamond to be so costly as a gem, much of its beauty and value are attributed on how it is cut. Until a rough diamond is cut, it actually lacks the appeal and charm that it has when it is polished and cut. The rough diamond looks like a lump of frosted crystal. Unlike the other gemstones whose attraction and allure are due primarily to their natural color, the colorless diamond is different because it produces color from light, capturing from outside the essence of its soul. If the diamond is not properly cut, its ability to refract light is not fully developed and the beauty of the diamond is left encapsulated in its core, its full potential restrained. The diamond achieves its fire and brilliance by the way it is cut, facetted and polished, but in order to project brilliance, the potential for brilliance must be there. The diamond possesses this potential.

In a rough diamond, an expert diamond cutter sees the latent grandeur and the promise of fire --- scintillating, sparkling pomp and splendor. When he examines a stone, he envisions the shape and mentally calculates the angles and the facets that will give brilliance and life into the rough stone.

Diamond cutting is generally assumed as having started in India. The reasons are obvious. Diamonds were first discovered in India and the Indians were the first to know that only diamonds can cut diamonds and only diamond powder, used as abrasive, can polish diamonds. They were the first to create simple facets by turning the stone on a small wheel dusted with diamond powder. The result of this initial efforts to create facets was not remarkable simply because, at that time, the Indians only facetted diamonds to conceal imperfections. Clear and lucid diamonds were left uncut and just polished to reveal their clarity. On the other hand, they also discovered the art of engraving on diamonds (or diamond carving) and came up with exquisitely engraved stones. This was because they learned that one face of the diamond crystal is soft compared to the other sides or faces that they can actually etch designs on it.

For the many centuries since 800 B.C. when diamonds were first discovered in India, the Indians had the prime advantage of working on diamonds. The magnificence of the diamond completely inspired artistry and craftsmanship such that they tried to invent ways to enhance its beauty as a jewel. And thus was invented the *point cut*, which was simply the natural octahedral form of the diamond polished all over. Simultaneously, the *table cut* was also invented which was the same as the point cut except that it had a flattened table on top and a similarly flattened culet at the bottom. These cuts were plain and uncomplicated attempts of the early Indian lapidaries to bring out more of the sparkle of the diamond. Although their attempts did little to really develop the capacity of the stone to show full brilliance, inventing both cuts was better than no cut at all. This certainly entailed artistic perseverance and incessant patience considering how hard the diamond is and yet to manually shape, cut and polish the stones as they did. Suffice it to say that the diamonds managed to sparkle because of their intrinsic brilliance and high quality. Crude in comparison to later efforts, the basic lapidary work already allowed the stones to catch and refract light. Up until now, those legendary Indian diamonds of great antiquity, although most have been recut for further brilliance, rank among the finest in world.

Due to factors that formed histories, mostly conquests, territorialities and trade relations, a great number of the Indian diamonds found their way to Europe. The Renaissance Period that started in Italy in the 14th century and gradually spread to other countries, brought forth a revival of interest in classical order and design ---- in art, literature and learning. Euclid's studies in geometry became the basis of "experimentations" in cuts, angles and geometrical planes on diamonds. These "experimentations" were sponsored by rich and extravagant patrons who were able and willing to purchase diamonds for the purpose. One such sponsor was Cardinal Mazarin who caused the rose cut design, a more facetted, far more brilliant version of the old point cut of India. Then in the 16th century, Vincenzo Peruzzi of Venice, cut the first diamond with the full 58 facets. Peruzzi was the first who purposely produced "fire" in the diamond. From then on, diamond cutters made improvements solely on Peruzzi's basic theme.

Diamond cutting plays a very important part in the diamond industry, particularly in the business of polished stones. It is an art and a science at the same time. It takes a keen eye, skilled craftsmanship and astute mathematical capability to create a good cut --- in shape, facets, proportion and symmetry. Today, the major cutting centers are New York, Antwerp, Tel Aviv and Bombay.

### The Diamond Cutting Process

The art of cutting the world's hardest mineral is a tedious and delicate process. Notwithstanding the emergence of sophisticated tools and machinery, the human touch still lords over the entire process thereby retaining its category as an art.

The process of cutting a diamond starts with *blocking*. Blocking involves getting a piece of rough diamond out of a major block which necessitates cleaving. Cleaving means splitting a diamond. In or-

der to be able to cleave a diamond, the diamond cutter first creates a groove with an industrial diamond. After a groove is made, the block is set on a holder and a steel wedge is inserted into the groove. The cutter then strikes a sharp blow on the steel wedge with a mallet, thus splitting the stone. If this were not a diamond, blocking will not be as stressful. But, because the material on hand is a diamond, care and skill are important since one bad blow can shatter the diamond to pieces.

A cutter cleaving a stone

35

The cutter's eye for perception is exercised to fore in blocking. Invincible and impervious a diamond is, like all stones, it has a "cleavage plane". Meaning, if you strike hard at a stone or drop it on a firm surface at a certain angle, it will possibly split along a cleavage line. It might not always happen, but the possibility is that it can happen because of the cleavage plane. The cutter must be able to perceive the position of the cleavage plane in order to determine where to split the stone or what to remove in the process of forming the gem.

Once the desired size is achieved, the diamond is ready for *sawing*. This step involves the use of the diamond-impregnated disk. The diamond-impregnated disk is a wheel made of cast iron and diamond powder. The disk turns at about 4,000 rpm (revolutions per minute) and will cut a one-carat rough diamond into its intended shape in four to eight hours. The diamond that is being shaped is inserted in a holder called dop. Sometimes, shaping the stone is done by *bruting* and involves roughly shaping two stones by rubbing one against the other. After the stone is shaped, it is ready for facetting.

*Facetting* is when the cutter either creates a fine masterpiece that can command a very good price in the market or come up with just a passable gem out of a good quality stone. This is where artistry, technique and skill are needed all together. The cutter creates

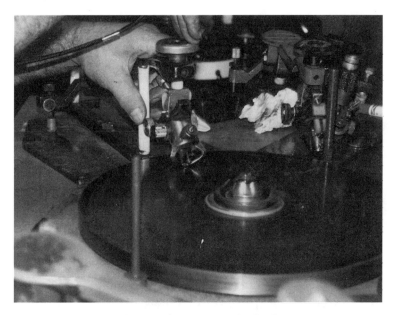

*Diamond Impregnated Wheel*

exact facets that should allow the maximum amount of light to enter the table and be refracted back to the top. The geometric angles must be able to refract the light and the dispersion should produce the fire and the glow that will burst and sparkle in a rainbow of colors. After all the facets are created according to the cutter's design, then the diamond is prepared for *polishing* which is the final step. Diamond dust is used as the abrasive to polish the diamond to further set off its brilliance and glow.

The basic risk that a diamond cutter takes is in his own skill. A small inaccuracy in the cut devalues the stone a hundredfold. For instance, a stone cleav-

37

age, which appears as a discernible line within the stone that breaks the pattern of brilliance, is a normal occurrence in the natural stone formation. If the stone is not big enough to necessitate cleaving or if the owner prefers not to split the stone, the cutter, in the process of sawing the stone into shape, should trim off the cleavage plane and yet must try to retain as much of the stone as possible. There should not be too much waste because of the common perception that the bigger the stone, the higher the price. The goal of every diamond cutter is to maximize brilliance while retaining maximum diamond weight. This, however, is a flexible standard because the significance of size or weight of the stone (carat) is diminished in factoring the market price if clarity or cut is obviously compromised.

The *dop* diamond holder, is used in facetting and polishing
the rough diamond.

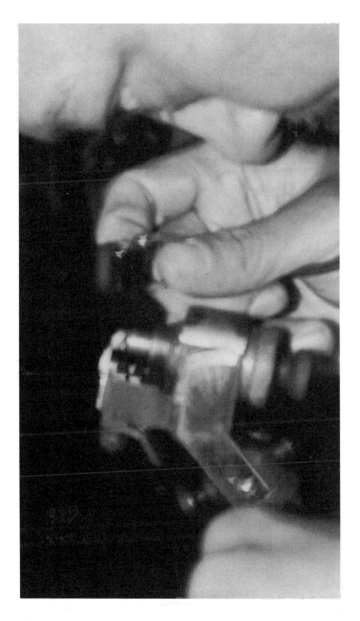

The author, *B.J. Tadena*, examining a diamond

## *Cutting : Form And Style*

In the trade, when cutting is discussed *per se*, it usually refers to the creation of facets. There are three basic forms or styles of cutting, namely: *step cut, brilliant cut* and *mixed cut.*

The *step cut* involves four rows of facets often elongated, four-sided and parallel to the girdle. Baguettes, emerald cut and princess cut are examples of step cuts but baguettes do not have as many facets as the latter two. Step cut can also be executed on triangular shapes.

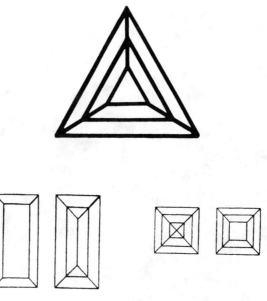

Examples of *step cuts*

The *brilliant cut* has kite-shaped facets created around the stone. Among the variations of this form are the rose cut, the old miner cut and the old European cut. The *single cut,* which is the style used for small round diamonds consisting of 18 facets, is also an example of this form. The old mine cut consists of 58 facets, a high crown, a small table and a large culet. It is square-shaped while the old European cut is round. Modern round brilliant cut, though still consisting of 58 facets, have a lower crown, a wider table and a pointed culet. This development allows for more brilliance and fire and the pointed culet has obliterated the illusion of a hole in the stone when viewed from the top.

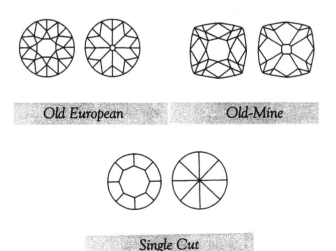

Old European          Old-Mine

Single Cut

Examples of *brilliant cuts*

41

The *mixed cut* consists of both step cut and brilliant cut. The pavilion is created with step cut facets while the crown is created with brilliant cuts. This form, however, is done more on other stones than on diamonds.

### *Seven Major Shapes*

There are seven major shapes to which a gemstone can be cut. Each has its own charm and allure. These are :

- *round brilliant cut* - the most popular shape and the most saleable. This shape has a total of 58 facets.

- *marquise* - much like the shape of a rice grain and is significantly and commonly used for engagement or wedding rings.

- *heart* - also frequently chosen for engagement rings, it is the most difficult shape to cut because of the grove at the center. Forming this shape takes a lot of skill and dexterity and any miscalculation will devalue or waste the stone altogether.

- *emerald* - rectangular with more facets applied.

- *princess* - squarish, usually a favorite of buyers as a center stone

42

- ***pear or teardrop*** - less popular among buyers and less expensive in comparison to other shapes except the oval.

- ***oval*** - like the teardrop, it is not also a popular choice of buyers and less expensive than other shapes.

**Basic Shapes of a Diamond**

### Intriguing Shapes and Styles

The following styles have emerged in the last 30 years. They are some of the forms or styles of cut that caught the attention of diamantaires and diamond lovers.

***The Radiant Cut.*** Designed and patented by Henry Grossbard of New York, this is a square or rectangular brilliant-cut with 70 facets. The corners are clipped-off like the emerald and princess cuts. This cut made its debut in Hong Kong in 1976.

***The Trielle.*** A brilliant-cut triangle designed by The Trillion Diamond Co., a subsidiary of LF Industries of New York, it was developed by Leon Finker in 1950's and patented in 1978. The Trielle is a registered trademark name. It may also be called ***Trillion.***

***The Quadrillion.*** Patented and registered as a trademark in 1981 by Ambar Diamonds of Los Angeles, this design features a brilliant-cut square diamond with 49 facets.

***The "144 Facets" Design.*** The round brilliant diamond with 58 facets is the result of the modern mathematical model out of the blueprint calculations of Marcel Tolkowski in 1919 and has become the pattern of brilliant cuts. The model was developed to be able

44

Examples of Shapes and Styles

*Radiant*

*Trilliant*

to reflect the most amount of light back to the top, or crown, and to the eye of the viewer. However, at that time, other considerations were not taken into account such as secondary reflections, oblique angles, among other factors. Today's technology and computerization gave birth to a pattern called "144 Facets" which was originally designed by the Huisman Brothers in the late

1960's and patented in 1986. Developed on the principle of a parabola, this particular design focuses the light into a concentrated zone. This has been proven efficient and effective in headlights, telescopes, spotlights and dish antennas. In diamonds, the parabolic shape of the "144 Facets" design allows the diamond to produce 32 percent more brilliance than the regular round with 58 facets. The design is executed with the creation of facets on the girdle and extra pavilion facets which meet with the girdle at a steeper angle. The result is an intriguing style which is more scintillating and desirable.

***Hearts And Arrows.*** Kinsaku Yamashita, a renowned Japanese diamantaire, invented a cut for diamonds that took the Japanese market by storm. He aptly named his artistic innovation as "Hearts And Arrows" because it has heart-shaped facets below the girdle instead of the pavilion facets. The facets are so precisely cut such that, when viewed from the top, the hearts look like arrowheads. This elaborate design, truly a visually poetic interpretation of love and romance rendered by way of the diamond, captured the Japanese market. Currently, 90% of engaged couples in Japan purchase diamond engagement rings and respond enthusiastically to the romantic design of the "Hearts And Arrows". Kinsaku Yamashita proceeded to register the name "Hearts And Arrows" as his trademark and incorporated his company under the name Heart And Arrow Company, Ltd. This move prohibited the

Hearts and Arrows

*"Hearts,"*
Bottom view

*"Arrows,"*
Top view

execution of the design without his permission and consequently limited the growth of the design in the diamond cutting industry.

As there is no limit to art, creativity, self-expression and individuality, there are no limits to contemporary designs and cuts. If the rough diamond is cut in extraordinary or unique shapes (star, fish, letters of the alphabet, logos etc.), these are called *fancy cuts*. Most gemologists and cutters in the industry also prefer to call *fancy* or *fancies* any shape other than the round brilliant cut. Thus, the princess cut or the oval are examples of fancy shapes or, simply called, *fancies* although their shapes are desirable and not unique. But for diamonds with unique and unusual shapes, like fish, snowman, fruit, logos, etc., it is presumed that such a unique shape is of emotional significance to the owner. Most uniquely designed fancies diminish the diamond's resale price. This is because the design is not common and may hold little or no significance to other people. Therefore, the market for resale is very limited. This is one reason why one should think also of the resale value of the rough diamond once the shape is determined for cutting. No one should ever take a diamond lightly. Frivolity commands a steep price.

# Part II

*Evaluating*

*and*

*Grading*

*Your Diamonds*

**(The Universal Standards Of The 4C's**
**:**
**Cut, Clarity, Color and Carat)**

# 5

## *Handy Instruments For*
## *Evaluation And Grading*

The diamond, a big investment in a small package. A diamond buyer should be perceptive enough to know how to examine what he is buying. Is it a natural diamond or a simulant? Is it really flawless or cosmetically altered? Is it rare-colored or is it a nail polish blush? Examining the diamond cannot be done just by looking at the stone with the naked eye because most inclusions, blemishes, hairline cracks, alterations, "cosmetic" enhancements or laser erasures cannot be seen without the proper instrument. Not even the most erudite and experienced diamantaire would evaluate or examine a stone without at least using a loupe. There are a number of instruments and equipments that are being used for evaluation and examination. These are used in diamond laboratories and dealerships. A number of these are small pocket instruments that dealers and jewelers use. These can also be used by anyone who is keenly interested and serious about the diamond that he is buying and prudent with the money that he is investing.

Before subjecting the diamond to close scrutiny, be sure that the diamond is clean. Thorough cleaning of the stone is essential because dust and other minute particles in the air could settle on the surface of the stone. These might be mistaken for inclusions under the microscope or through the loupe. Steam cleaning is very good for most gems. Another method of cleaning is by dipping the stone in a container of rubbing alcohol and gently stroking it with a soft brush. Dry the stone with a clean cloth or paper towel. Avoid handling the stone with your fingers because fingers can leave prints and smudges on the stone. Use tweezers to handle the stone. Next, be sure that you have good overhead lighting. Overhead lighting should be white, not colored.

- The *loupe* is the basic instrument often used to look into the diamond. It is a hand magnifier that has a 10X or 18X magnification, magnifying the stone ten times or 18 times its size. With a lot of practice and experience, a loupe can tell even the amateur a great deal. It can help determine whether a stone is a natural diamond, synthetic or just plain glass. It can also identify characteristic inclusions, blemishes or cracks. The loupe, however, is limited to show only up to SI (Slight Inclusion) to Imperfect $I_3$.

- *Tweezers* or a diamond holder is a basic essential because of the size of the stone. It is just logical to see that it is more convenient to hold the stone with the tweezers than with your fingers while examining the stone. Using tweezers will also avoid leaving smudges on the stone.

A 10-power triplet *loupe*

- A *diamond tester* like the GIA Gem Pocket Diamond Tester is a battery operated instrument that measures heat conductivity of the stone. Considering the principle that diamonds conduct heat better that any imitation stone, this tester has a metal probe that is pressed on the stone. The meter then shows whether the stone is a diamond or an imitation.

- In this age of technology, even the conventional weight scale caught up with the times. A *pocket carat scale* will readily determine the weight of the stone in carats. Light, pocketsize and battery-operated, it comes in handy especially when carat becomes the final determinant of price.

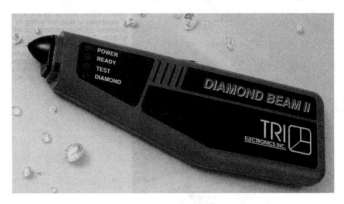

Diamond Tester

Pocket Carat Scale

- A *master color stone* is a guide to color grading and evaluation. It consists of a diamond that corresponds to each of the five different color grades in the color grading scale from D (colorless) to Z (light yellow). The diamond to be examined should

Master Color Stone

be compared to the master stones to determine the exact color grade. In examining the diamond, this should be held against a non-reflective white background, usually a plain white folded paper.

- The *binocular microscope* is a two-lens microscope used to observe more clearly the same items that are observed with the loupe. Its capability and power however are of much higher magnification that is especially useful in differentiating natural gems from synthetic stones and to detect treatments done on the diamond. This equipment is also most useful in determining table "spread" measurement vis-à-vis proportion. It determines clarity grade of diamonds from $VS_2$ (Very Slight Inclusion) to VVS

55

(Very Very Slight Inclusion) and IF (Internally Flawless) that a loupe cannot do. The binocular microscope may not be as handy as the loupe but dealers should have one. This is to distinguish precisely the natural diamond from the well-made simulant, the clear and flawless stone from the treated.

Binocular Microscope

*Note:*

Since the loupe is the handiest and the most frequently used instrument that even the average consumer can use, it is believed of greater service to inform the reader how to use the loupe properly. The loupe should be held about one inch away from the left eye (because the left eye is assumed more powerful than the right). Peer into the loupe with both eyes open and adjust the distance of the stone to get the correct focus. Practice focusing first on any item that you want to see up close --- the pores of the skin, a strand of hair or a glass marble. Rotate the item slowly. Hold the loupe at varying distances until focusing becomes easy. When you become comfortable with the loupe, you are now ready to focus on the diamond or any gemstone.

The *loupe* is a handy instrument for
both the jeweler and the buyer.

The diamond is a highly priced commodity and for this reason, it has become important for diamond buyers to learn how to inspect the merchandise. One should not be embarrassed to examine the stone. The buyer has every right to know the diamond more than the dealer's description and more than its showcased beauty and seduction. You might as well know whether all that fire and sparkle is real.

# 6

*Cut*

In evaluating and grading the diamond, the criteria is based on a set of industry standards and parameters involving the 4 C's ---- *cut, color, clarity and carat.*

Cut refers to the proportions and finish of the facetted diamond. To jewelers, cut can also mean the shape of the stone (i.e., round, marquise, oval) or the cutting style (brilliant cut, step cut, mixed cut). The only one among the 4C's that is affected by human intervention, cut alone frees the fire and the brilliance in the diamond. It is cut alone that releases the hypnotic seduction of this magnificent gem.

Most diamond buyers are more concerned with the clarity, color and carat weight of the diamond and would tend to overlook cut proportions and symmetry. Since shapes and cutting styles have been discussed in Chapter 4, this chapter will delve on proportion, symmetry and other factors that are influenced by the cut of the diamond.

When discussing proportion, the concern is on how the stone is proportionately cut in relation to its diameter. The diameter of the stone is the measurement of the girdle (the rim that separates the top from the bottom). The primary factors to consider here are the *table percentage* and *depth percentage.*

*Table percentage* is the figure that shows the measurement of the table in proportion to the girdle. The table is the flat, top facet on the crown through which most of the light enters and exits. The ideal proportion of the table is 53 to 60 % of the diameter of the stone. Beyond 60 %, some trade buyers will consider the table too spread out. This is important only in stones that are one-half carat or more because the table proportion is more pronounced in bigger stones.

The *depth percentage* is the measurement of the depth of the stone. The ideal percentage is 59 to 61%, meaning, that the depth must be 59 to 61 % from crown to culet in perpendicular ratio to the diameter. A low 58% and a high 62 % is acceptable. More than 62 % or less than 58 % is considered inexcusable workmanship and outside of trade standards and parameters.

In the same breath as the depth percentage is the *pavilion depth.* If the pavilion is cut too deep, light will escape through the side of the pavilion. If it is too shallow, light will escape through the pavilion. The ideal pavilion depth percentage is between 41 to 48% of the girdle diameter. Having a pavilion depth within the ideal percentage enables a more effective refraction and the stone is indeed more brilliant.

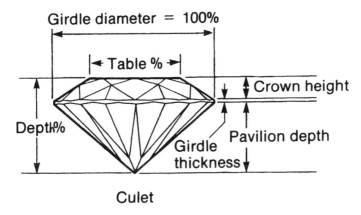

Margins of proportion of a well-cut *round brilliant diamond*

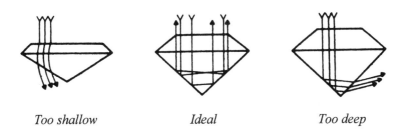

*Too shallow*          *Ideal*          *Too deep*

Pavilion Depth

Once set, there is one aspect of the diamond that is rather difficult to ascertain ---- the workmanship on the girdle. In describing a well-cut, well-facetted girdle, it is easier to point out what a girdle should not be. A well-cut, well-facetted girdle should not be too thick such that the diamond looks smaller than its carat weight. A thick girdle results in a smaller table that

61

affects, not only its visual size, but also its capability to refract light properly. The girdle should not also be too thin such that it chips off easily and is difficult to set. Likewise, the girdle should not be slanted nor bearded, as these too are marks of poor craftsmanship. As mentioned before, it may be difficult to see the girdle once the diamond is set, but some settings will allow a peek at the girdle.

*Girdle* proportions. Illustration (b) is a well-cut, well-facetted girdle.

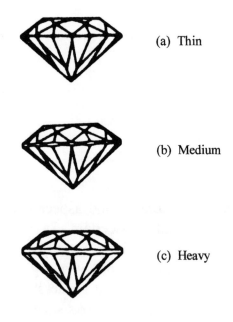

(a) Thin

(b) Medium

(c) Heavy

Other measurements to consider are the *crown angle* and the *pavilion angle*. The crown angle should be cut at a 35° angle. Crown angle is measured in terms of the 8 bezel facets, those kite-shaped facets on the crown. An angle less than this will give the diamond a "spread -cut" appearance Above 35° will give a smaller table and will give the stone a smaller appearance than its real carat weight. Pavilion angle must be cut at a 41° angle. Pavilion angle is measured in terms of the 8 pavilion facets or lower bezel facets. If the pavilion angle is not cut at the proper angle, there is a certain loss of sparkle. Both the crown and the pavilion angles must be cut properly in order for the light to enter the crown from all directions and directed to the pavilion facets for maximum reflection. The light then exits from the stone through the crown bouncing off at angles that produces brilliance and fire without obstruction from improperly cut angles. This constitutes the essential diamond material data.

**Ideal Cut Diamond**

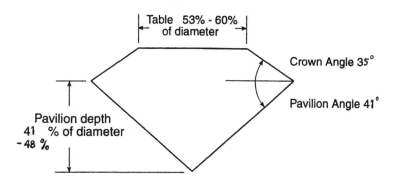

The proper degree angles of the crown and pavilion angles in relation to the table percentage and the pavilion depth percentage.

Symmetry is the balance or beauty of form and proportion and must not be taken lightly since the obvious lack of it devalues or destroys a stone. The sense of symmetry must be an innate characteristic of a diamond cutter and should reflect on his creations. Therefore, a well-cut stone should be symmetrical or as nearly symmetrical as could be. Balance and symmetry in cut and proportions determine the amount of light that enters the diamond. Balance and symmetry determine how light bursts into an arresting rainbow of colors that catches the eye of the beholder. This play of light that causes brilliance and life is what the consumer gets out of a well-cut, symmetrical stone ---- the encapsulated beauty of a sparkling star. One sees the grandeur in the play of light but cannot exactly explain what causes it. Is it the angles? The facets? The shape? Knowing your diamond is knowing that it is the careful and intricate execution of the cut that allows the entry of light into the stone. It is the symmetry of proportions that allow the arresting brilliance of the stone to shine and hypnotize the captive beholder.

### *The Ideal Cut*

Sometime in 1919, Marcel Tolkowsky came up with a mathematical calculation of the best angles and proportions of cutting that will allow the optimum amount of life (then defined as the light returned to the eye) and fire ( burst of colors) in a diamond. Before this, cutters and polishers of the time only had Euclid's geometric formulae that are, safe to say, the basis of all studies in geometry ---- including Tolkowsky's. While Tolkowsky's measurements initiated the importance of precision cutting leading to the notion of an "ideal cut," it is a highly debated issue in the industry. The question is whether *the* ideal cut, with its smaller table, causes more brilliance in the stone than other cuts. It was recently found that there are other types of cut and varying proportions within the cut that can produce equal to or more brilliance than the so called "ideal cut".

### Other Factors To Consider

Other factors have to be considered in cutting the diamond that would enhance fire and life.

- Dispersion is when light enters the stone and breaks up into colored rays. It is what may be considered as the fire in the stone and is achieved through proper cutting of angles and facets. Dispersion is the resultant effect of refraction.

- Refraction is when a ray or a wave of light bends as it enters the stone obliquely. When refraction is good, the wave of light will disperse and come back to the viewer's eye. Gemologists use the refractometer in order to measure the refractive index of a stone. The higher the refractive index, the more lustrous and radiant the stone will be ---- if the cut is good. A well-cut stone should have a pavilion that is well executed. If the cut of the stone is too shallow, the light will not bend, or refract, properly. Instead, the light will pass out or leak through the pavilion and create a "window" that can be viewed from the top of the stone. Because of this, the stone may appear dull.

### Some Resultant Defects Due To Bad Cutting

◆ *fisheye* -- an appearance in a diamond that is apparent from the top and looks like a flat circle with a hole. This is caused by a shallow pavilion.

◆ *nailhead* -- an appearance of a dark center in a diamond seen from the top that is caused by a pavilion that was cut too deep.

◆ *bow tie* -- this is seen in fancy-shaped diamonds and is caused by incorrect cut proportions.

◆ *black cross* -- this is seen from the top like a layered black cross. This is also due to incorrect cut proportions on emerald cuts and princess cuts.

◆ *bearding or girdle fringes* -- these are whisker-like roughness around the girdle that is the result of hasty cutting or improper polishing. Repolishing the stone may be able to remedy the situation. If it does not, facetting the girdle will solve the problem.

- ◆ *nick* -- a small chip along the girdle that may be caused by the wear and tear of a diamond whose girdle is too thin. This is usually seen at the point where two facet edges meet (making a "bruised corner"). This can be corrected through repolishing by creating an extra facet.

- ◆ *pits or cavities* -- seen on the table facet, these small holes lower the value of the stone considerably. If they are deep, the stone will have to be recut resulting in a lower carat weight and could jeopardize the symmetry of the stone.

- ◆ *abraded or rough culet* -- this occurs when the culet is either chipped or the cut is not smooth. In modern-cut stones, the culet is reduced to the size of a point and thus, becomes sensitive to chipping. When the culet is chipped, there is an appearance of a window, which can be seen from the top. This affects the brilliancy of the stone.

- ◆ *polishing lines* -- this is the result of a badly maintained polishing wheel. A minor flaw if it is not obvious, the lines will not devalue the stone if they appear on the sides of the pavilion.

As stated in the previous chapter, diamond cutting is a happy blending of art and science. In today's high technology and computerized calibration of machines and equipments, precision is a given factor. One can almost assume that, with the equipment calibrated to perfect or near-perfect settings, a perfect cut or exact facets can be produced. That is cold science ---- as cold as the diamond in the rough. Because of the human factor in the process of cutting the stone, art remains. Although the human factor is what causes most of the errors, it is the touch and the feel of human intervention that makes diamond cutting an art. Man gives this craft its heart and breath. It is man's participation in the creation of its brilliance that the diamond, in turn, returns its own expression of beauty and fire and life.

# 7

*Clarity*

Clarity refers to the clearness of the stone. Some centuries back, the clarity of the diamond was measured in terms of its crystal-clear purity compared to water. A diamond of high purity and fineness was once said to be *"a diamond of the first water"*. *River* and *extra river* used to denote diamonds of the finer qualities. Thus, a diamond of the highest grade was said to be *extra river*. Those were the times when facetting was simple, if not crude, and the water of the rivers was clear, pure, and unpolluted with industrial wastes as it is now.

A diamond is formed under the earth's crust. During its formation, other minerals, uncrystallized carbon molecules, specks of dirt or other matters foreign to its nature often become embedded within the rough diamond. These are called *inclusions* and they can be solid, liquid or gaseous matters that may or may not be removed in the process of cutting. Most gemstones, including diamonds, have inclusions. Inclusions may also be internal stress fractures or imperfections in the structural arrangement of crystallized carbon. Cleavage planes or cracks are internal flaws and they are also called inclusions. Inclusions are not often visible to the naked eye but can be seen

69

through the use of the loupe with good overhead lighting and better observed by using a binocular microscope. Inclusions greatly affect the value of the diamond because they detract the flow of light waves and lessen the brilliance of the stone. The more obvious and centered (or near the center) the inclusion is, the lower the value of the stone. If the inclusion is slight, located more along the fringes of the girdle or does not affect the strength of the stone, the devaluation of the stone is not as much. The types of inclusions are: feathers, cleavages or cracks, uncrystallized carbon, tiny black pinpoints, included crystals and clouds of white pinpoints.

A *blemish* is any external imperfection that is seen on the surface of the diamond. It mars perfection and affects the clarity of the stone. However, since blemishes are external, the situation can often be remedied through repolishing. Recutting may be resorted to if the blemish is serious but this will lessen the carat weight and jeopardize symmetry. The types of blemishes are: natural (unpolished part of a diamond), polishing lines, scratches, chips, bearding (whisker-like roughness along the girdle) and fracture (a crack on the surface of the diamond).

The Gemological Institute of America (GIA) established a standard grading scale for evaluating clarity of diamonds:

◆ *Flawless* **(FL)**
Free from inclusions. Free from blemishes. Flawless diamonds are expensive, rare and are usually collectors' items. Flawless diamonds are a pleasure to look at and are seldom mounted in jewelry.

◆ *Internally Flawless* **(IF)**
Free from inclusions under binocular microscope observation but may have slight blemishes. Also rare and expensive and seldom mounted in jewelry.

◆ *Very, Very Slight Inclusion(s)* **(VVS$_1$ and VVS$_2$)**
Only minute inclusions or blemishes are allowed in this grade level under binocular microscope observation. The stone may be recut *if* the inclusion is near the surface and if doing so would upgrade the clarity level of the stone and increase its value without jeopardizing carat weight and symmetry. If the beauty of the stone is jeopardized in any way, it is best to leave the inclusions alone. The stone in this level is considered high quality and expensive.

◆ *Very Slight Inclusion(s)* **(VS$_1$ and VS$_2$)**
Only small inclusions under binocular microscope observation which may even be difficult to see under 10X magnification of the loupe. Recutting the stone in this category seldom upgrades its clarity level. Still considered high quality and selected for top-grade jewelry.

◆ *Slight Inclusions* **(SI$_1$)**
More or larger inclusions or blemishes under 10X magnification. Inclusions may include small

71

cracks, cleavages, fractures and carbon. SI diamonds are "eye clean", meaning, that the inclusions cannot be seen by the naked eye. The stones in this level are considered good quality and are often what many jewelry stores sell.

♦ *Slight Inclusions* (SI$_2$)
More or larger inclusions or blemishes under 10X magnification, but most of which are visible to the naked eye.

♦ *Imperfect* (I$_1$)
Many inclusions and blemishes which are visible to the naked eye when viewed up close. Considered commercial grade diamonds.

♦ *Imperfect* (I$_2$)
Many inclusions and blemishes visible from a distance of about 12 inches to 18 inches. The stone appears cloudy and lifeless. Considered low commercial grade.

♦ *Imperfect* (I$_3$)
Very many inclusions and blemishes visible from a distance of more than 18 inches. The stone appears dull. Low commercial grade.

In discussing clarity characteristics of the diamond, some of the blemishes that are taken into account have been discussed in the previous chapter. This is because the diamond is judged and graded based on the interaction of the 4C's factors and other influences that give it beauty, brilliance and life. Since cut is the only one among the 4C's that is affected by human intervention, some of the defects of bad cutting procedures affect the clarity of the diamond as blemishes, such as nicks, pits, scratches and polishing lines. These are often superficial and can be remedied through repolishing.

GIA-Based Clarity Grading Scale

| IF | VVS-1 | VVS-2 | VS-1 | VS-2 | SI-1 | SI-2 | SI-3 | I-1 | I-2 | I-3 |
|---|---|---|---|---|---|---|---|---|---|---|
| Flawless | Very very slight inclusions | | Very slight inclusions | | Slight Inclusions | | | Imperfect | | |

*Note:* *The Clarity Grading Scale starts at internally flawless (IF) because flawless diamonds (FL) do not have any inclusion or blemish even as viewed through a binocular microscope. FL diamonds are pure and extremely rare and in a league of their own.*

*Laser drill holes* are man-made inclusions that must be noted here. Laser drilling is a treatment that removes black spots of carbon from the inside of the stone through the use of a laser beam. The laser beam, however, creates a tunnel from the surface of the diamond to the place where the black spots used to be. The process is supposed to improve the appearance of the stone but the laser drill holes, which look like white suspended threads, sometimes make it worse.

The GIA first introduced the grading system in the later part of the 1920's. This has undergone modifications to satisfy or closely satisfy the needs of the industry. Establishing a grading system was not exactly easy because human subjectivity made grading inconsistent. Evaluating diamonds should be done by experienced and trained graders because grading and evaluating requires a lot of practice and exposure. Our objective in this book, however, is to make the regular buyer be informed of what to look for and to make his own objective estimation. The regular buyer should be informed enough in order not to be taken in by unscrupulous sellers and jewelers. If an SI diamond is available at the price of an imperfect, by all means, get the SI! Do not be fooled into buying or investing on an imperfect stone because it is practically impossible to resell. It can be bought from you at a dirt-cheap price that speaks of bad investment, unless you bought it at dirt-cheap price too. Whereas beauty is in the eye of the beholder, let your diamond be beautiful also in the eyes of others.

# Examples of Inclusions in Each Clarity Grade
## VS1 (very slight inclusions)

One cloud of pinpoints under table. One natural. One long extra facet. One very small cleavage extending from girdle.

Very small inclusion under table edge. Two naturals

Small feather near girdle. Nick on girdle. Group of pinpoints under table. Straight grain lines through crown; curved lines on pavilion.

Three knots; one on table, two on pavilion. One large extra facet.

Two poinpoints under table. One long scratch on table. One natural. Two extra faces on the crown and pavilion.

One small "carbon spot" under table edge. Two small included crystal under star facet. One pinpoint under table. One natural.

Two small opaque inclusions under table area.

Two small included crystals. One pinpoint under table.

## Examples of Inclusions in Each Clarity Grade
## VS2 (very slight inclusions)

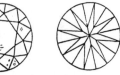

Two small included crystals.
One extra facet. One small
cleavage near girdle.
Two naturals.

Several cloudy streaks under
table. One included crystal.
Several pinpoints. One small
cleavage under crown.

Pinpoint under table. Two
cleavages on pavilion. One
extra facet and one natural;
same area.

One fairly large irregular
inclusion on crown. One
natural on girdle.

Two small cleavages on
crowns near girdle. Two cleavages on pavilion. Tiny fissure
on upper-girdle facet.

Many extra facets. Three nicks.
One natural. Two "carbon
spots" near girdle. One included crystal. One pinpoint.

Two large nicks, several small
inclusions and one area of
poor polish on table. Extra
facet, two small cleavages and
twinning lines on pavilion.

Small cleavage and two inclusions under table. Two extra
facets on crown; one on pavilion. Natural on pavilion; many
scratches on junction.

76

# Examples of Inclusions in Each Clarity Grade.
## SI1 (slight inclusions)

  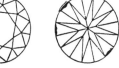

Three small cleavages. "Carbon or black spot." Row of pinpoints.

Two large nicks. One natural and one extra facet. Three large indented naturals.

One fairly large irregular inclusion. Large nick on girdle. Abraded culet.

Very rough area around girdle edge. Three small cleavages. Two naturals.

Nick in center of table. Three extra facets. Large group of pinpoints with cleavage. One natural.

Two cleavages. One small "carbon spot." One included crystal with several pinpoints. One extra facet on crown. One natural.

Two groups of scratches on table. One natural. One cleavage. Fracture on culet. Series of nicks.

One group and several individual included crystals. One extra facet. One natural.

# Examples of Inclusions in Each Clarity Grade.
## SI2 (slight inclusions)

One group of irregular opaque inclusions. One natural.

Four prominent cloudy areas. Three naturals.

One medium feather. One small cleavage. Several irregular inclusions. One nick. Several pinpoints. One chip on girdle. One natural.

Three small feathers. One natural. At least five small cleavages. One included crystal with group of pinponts.

Two cleavages. One feather under table. Two naturals. One included crystal.

One indented, unpolished area on table. One cloud of needle inclusions near girdle. Two cleavages. One feather. One included crystal.

One long narrow cleavage starting at girdle. Several extra facets. One natural.

One thin cleavage near girdle. One small cloud under table edge. Two naturals.

78

# Examples of Inclusions in Each Clarity Grade.
## I1 (imperfect)

Large "feathery" type of sepa-
ration. Girdle outline inter-
rupted by a natural. Large
natural, indented, on pavilion.

Long thin cleavage across
crown facets. At least
five other small cleavages.
Several included crystals.
One pinpoint.

One large irregular inclusion
complex under table.
One small "carbon spot."
One natural.

Large included crystal
with three cleavages. Three
smaller included crystals.
Two extra facets.

One severe nick, or fissure
on pavilion. Several large
and small included crystals
under table.

Several small cleavages.
Several feathers. Large
elongated included crystal.
Included distorted
octahedron. One natural.

Two parallel planes of minute
white inclusions. Two areas of
roughness on girdle edge.

Large group of small feathers.
Two naturals.

79

## Examples of Inclusions in Each Clarity Grade.
## I2 (imperfect)

# Examples of Inclusions in Each Clarity Grade.
## I3 (imperfect)

# 8

*Color*

Unlike what is commonly perceived, diamonds do cover a wide range of colors but it is the rare colorless diamond that is most sought after. Colorless diamonds are mostly desired because they allow the most reflection of light.

Despite popular misconceptions about diamonds being colorless, most diamonds are tinted with color and colorless diamonds are hard to come by. The most common color is pale yellow or a *tint* of yellow caused by varying amounts of nitrogen present in the crystal structure. Others may have a *tint* of blue caused by tiny amounts of boron, while others may be brown, green or gray. Diamonds with a *tint* of color are less valuable than colorless diamonds but they should not be confused with *natural fancy colored diamonds*. Natural fancy colored diamonds are <u>strongly colored</u>, rare and very expensive. Among these are blue, pink, green, red and canary yellow. Black, where graphite is present, may be considered in this category because it is also very rare. An example of a natural colored diamond is the famous *Hope Diamond,* which used to be called the *French Blue* before it was recut and acquired by Henry Thomas Hope. Other examples are the *Dresden Green*, the intense yellow *Shephard* and the black *Star of Amsterdam.*

As already mentioned, the common tint in most diamond gemstones is yellow. This explains why the Gemological Institute of America (GIA) developed and established the internationally accepted color grading system based on the determination of the lack of yellow in a diamond. *The Color Grading Scale* uses the alphabetical letters to indicate the level of yellow tint in a diamond in comparison to a set of pre-graded master stones.

A diamond should be compared to the set of *Master Stones* to determine its color grade.

The Color Grading Scale starts with the D, E and F (colorless), which are the highest and the most expensive because they are rare, onwards to Z (the more yellow), which are the less expensive. It is possible that the average consumer might not even notice the difference in color of a mounted diamond within the grades G to J because the increasing variance is really very slight. The difference in color within the grades N to Z however, is obvious and the buyer should pay a lot less. For instance, a diamond with an R color could cost ten times less than a D color assuming all other aspects being equal. *Diamonds that are strongly colored yellow (Z+) are categorized as fancies and are priced differently. Their price increases as their colors intensify.*

| D | E | F | G | H | I | J | K | L | M |
|---|---|---|---|---|---|---|---|---|---|
| *Colorless* | | | *Near colorless* | | | | *Faint Yellow* | | |

**GIA Color Grading Scale**

*Note:* *For brevity, the Scale is only up to grade M to match the author's Price Guide. The description for N to Z is very light to light yellow. There is no grade above D.*

**How to Determine Color Grade**

In determining the color grade of diamonds, the evaluation must be done by a trained and experienced professional. Be it as it may, at least you are not going to the jewelry store knowing nothing about color grading.

The jeweler should have the following on hand: a set of Master Stones, a non-reflective white paper or white plastic grading tray and a good diffused light source (fluorescent lamp). The stone must be placed on the white paper or tray and must be compared to the Master Stones. No matter how good the jeweler's memory is, it is difficult and impossible to recall precise colors, much more for very slight variations in tint. The stone under scrutiny must be clean and so with the Master Stone.

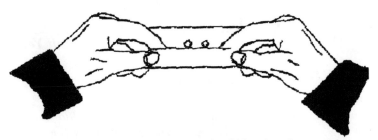

The diamond and the *master stone* should be placed on a white non-reflective paper or plastic tray

Compare the diamond from both sides of the master. It is possible for its color to be lighter on the left or the right because of refraction and the light source. The surroundings can also affect the color because of reflection, e.g., the color of your clothes, the air quality, the time of day. Consider also the size of the stone. If the master is smaller than the diamond being graded, the larger stone will appear darker because the color is easier to see in bigger stones. It would be good to note that the color of a diamond that is already mounted on jewelry can only be estimated because the color of the metal can influence the color of the stone.

Fluorescence is a characteristic or property of a substance to produce light while it is being acted upon by radiant energy such as ultraviolet rays or x-rays. Some diamonds have this characteristic. In some, the fluorescence is strong enough that it reacts to the ultraviolet component of daylight. The effect is a hazy milky appearance that may affect the color grade of the diamond.

## Color Treatments

I cannot end this chapter without touching on color enhancements or color treatments. Enhancing the rainbow and intensifying the color of nature is indeed very tempting. And so it is with diamonds. Although colorless diamonds are more expensive in their rarity and pureness, natural colored fancies are as expensive. It is not surprising then that some jewelers resort to color treatments to make an expensive rare canary yellow out of a least expensive grade Q. A strongly colored green out of a low-grade brownish tinted diamond, maybe?

Believe it or not, some color treatments are legitimate and acceptable trade practices. Jewelers and dealers, however, are required by the Federal Trade Commission to disclose the color enhancements and other gem treatments to the public. These treatments should not be done to deceive the buyer into believing that the stone is a natural colored fancy that should command a higher price.

Color treatments are done on most commercial stones to either improve on the color or to lessen the visual impact of inclusions. Stones may be irradiated (exposure to radiation), lasered or surface coated (painted). Diamonds that are subjected to irradiation treatment retain the color permanently. The irradiated stones look like the very expensive natural fancies but they tend to appear metallic. The process is done through a cyclotron and, even if the color stays permanent and stable (will not fade through time and sunlight exposure), the treatment can be detected by reputable gem laboratories with the use of the spectroscope.

Although lasering is not done to enhance color, it is done to remove unsightly black spots or black inclusions from diamonds. In a way, it is also a color enhancement since the objective is to make the stone appear clearer but not necessarily more brilliant. The laser cuts a hole towards the inclusion. After this, the diamond is soaked in an acid formula to remove or erase the black area. Because of the absence of the inclusion from the naked eye of the buyer, the gem may be sold as a diamond of higher grade by an unscrupulous jeweler or dealer to a trusting or unknowing buyer. Again, the Federal Trade Commission requires that lasering must be disclosed. Otherwise, the dealer is committing fraud. Acceptable as it may be, lasering can be detected by any gem laboratory and indicated in their certificate of analysis.

Painting, or euphemistically called surface coating, is sometimes done on diamonds to enhance their color. Lately, natural fancies of red and intensely pink diamonds from the Argyle Mines of Australia have commanded exorbitant price ranges. Once, a 3.25-carat pink Argyle diamond sold for $1.65 million at an auction. So, the temptation to do surface coating is just too much to resist. But solvents can often remove surface coatings just as easily as acetone or nail polish remover can remove nail polish. In fact, surface coating is mostly nail polish blush that may be applied to the stone prior to mounting. Just the same, this kind of treatment has to be disclosed because it is clearly an attempt to defraud if there is no disclosure.

There are other ways to enhance the color or the beauty of a diamond, especially if the stone is of lower quality. Logically, mounted diamonds are easy to "make-over" because their metal casting provide a good cover for the pavilion. Some diamonds are coated at the pavilion to make the stone look less yellow. Sometimes the girdle is dubbed with minute amount of ink to improve the color of the stone.

Color grading can often be subjective. The establishment of the Color Grading Chart by the GIA can, at least, minimize disagreements over the slight nuances of color. Just be reminded, though, that in shopping for a diamond, it is better to compare prices first and demand for a certificate of grade analysis coming from a gem laboratory. The certificate may still be the grader's opinion, but it is a documented opinion by which the grader and the dealer stand. It is a document by which they stake their professional integrity and their business.

# 9

How many times have we heard the question "How big is your diamond? Half carat? One carat?" "Oh it's a rock! No, a boulder!" When talk veers toward diamonds, the first question is always on the carat weight and with it is, of course, its size. This is expected because, among the 4C's, carat weight is the only one that the regular consumer can see based on the size of the diamond. With his limited knowledge, he can make a rough estimate of the carat weight of a particular stone. Maybe he can and maybe not. Show him a one carat diamond and this will stick. Show him a good cut and he might yet forget.

Carat is a unit of weight measurement for precious stones, including pearls. One carat is equivalent to 200 milligrams (1 ct) and there are five carats to a gram (5 ct). It is the easiest among the 4C's to determine because it is exact and objective. The term carat originated in ancient times when precious stones were weighed against the carob bean. It was the French who first started to adopt the metric carat in 1907. Spain followed also in 1907 and other countries subsequently. In 1914, Great Britain, the United States, Holland and Belgium simultaneously adopted the metric carat. After this, more countries followed. Today

91

the metric carat is the internationally accepted measure of weight for gems and precious stones. This should not be confused with *karat, which* is the standard of weight measurement for gold.

The diamond industry has its own lingo and its expression of carats in terms of points is one worth knowing. It is easier to say *five points* or a *five pointer* than to say five one-hundredths of a carat. The equivalent of the carat weight in points follows:

| | | |
|---:|:---:|:---:|
| 100 pts | = | 1 ct |
| 50 pts | = | 0.50 ct |
| 1 pt | = | 0.01 ct |
| ½ pt | = | 0.005 ct |
| 25 pts | = | quarter ct |
| 20 pts | = | 0.2 ct. |

The Rapaport Diamond Report issues a regular list of diamond prices for the industry based on the instituted direction of De Beers. The Rapaport Diamond Report has established weight categories for diamonds and this system facilitates its determination of entries into its monthly price list. Low quality diamonds do not have as much of a high increase in price from one weight category to the next unlike high quality diamonds. The price jumps of high quality diamonds are more significant. The bigger they are, the higher the increase in price such that there is usually a big jump in price from .99 ct to 1 ct. After all, .99 ct is still not 1 ct and having a 1 ct diamond is something else.

| Weight Categories for Diamonds | | |
|---|---|---|
| 0.01- 0.03 ct | 0.30 - 0.37 ct | 0.96 - 0.99 ct |
| 0.04 - 0.07 ct | 0.38 - 0.45 ct | 1.00 - 1.49 ct |
| 0.08 - 0.14 ct | 0.46 - 0.49 ct | 1.50 - 1.99 ct |
| 0.15 - 0.17 ct | 0.50 - 0.69 ct | 2.00 - 2.49 ct |
| 0.18 - 0.22 ct | 0.70 - 0.89 ct | 2.50 - 2.99 ct |
| 0.23 - 0.29 ct | 0.90 - 0.95 ct | 3.00 -3.99 ct |

Carat Weight Categories for Diamonds based on
the *Rapaport Diamond Report*.

There are two ways of estimating the carat weight of a diamond: by using a diamond weight estimator or with the use of the diamond weight estimation formulas developed by the GIA. The Diamond Weight Estimation Formulas are formulas used to extrapolate the estimated weight of the diamond on the assumption that the proportions are good. A 2% weight correction margin must be added for slightly thick girdles. For thick to extremely thick girdles, 4% to 10% weight correction margins must be added. First, determine the measurement of the stone with a gauge. Then, compute for its estimated weight using the formulas in the given chart. Multiply 2% to the product to get the weight correction margin. Add the weight correction margin to the estimated weight. The sum total is the actual carat weight. For example, take a round brilliant cut with a diameter of 6.74 mm and with a depth of 3.75 mm:

1)    $(6.74)^2$ X 3.75 X .0061=1.039 (Estimated Carat Weight)

**Get 2% of Estimated Carat Weight to get the Margin for Weight Correction:**

2)    1.039 X .02 (or 2%)=.0207 (Weight Correction Margin)

**Add the Weight Correction Margin to the Estimated Carat Weight:**

3)    1.039 + .0207= 1.059 Actual Carat Weight

The diamond weight estimator provides the jeweler or the buyer with the carat weight based on the diameter of the diamond in millimeters. It is also assumed that its proportions are good. The following diagram may be used also to estimate carat weight based on the diameter of round brilliant-cut diamonds.

| Diamond Weight Estimation Formulas | |
|---|---|
| **Round Brilliant** | Average diameter$^2$ x depth x .0061 |
| **Oval Brilliant** | Average diameter$^2$ x depth x .0062 (avg. diameter = L + W ÷ 2) |
| **Heart-Shape Brilliant** | Length x width x depth x .0059 |
| **Square Brilliant** | Length x width x depth x .0085 |
| **Triangular Brilliant** | Length x width x depth x .0057 |
| **Pear Shape** | Length x width x depth x .00615 if length/width ratio is 1.25:1<br>Length x width x depth x .0060 if length/width ratio is 1.50:1<br>Length x width x depth x .00575 if length/width ratio is 2.00:1 |
| **Marquise** | Length x width x depth x .00565 if length/width ratio is 1.50:1<br>Length x width x depth x .00580 if length/width ratio is 2.00:1<br>Length x width x depth x .00585 if length/width ratio is 2.50:1 |
| **Emerald Cut** | Length x width x depth .0080 if length/width ratio is 1.00:1<br>Length x width x depth x .0092 if length/width ratio is 1.50:1<br>Length x width x depth x .0100 if length/width ratio is 2.00:1 |

*GIA Diamond Weight Estimation Formulas*

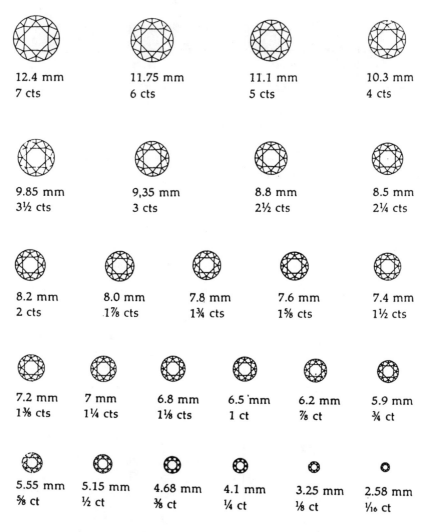

| | | | |
|---|---|---|---|
| 12.4 mm<br>7 cts | 11.75 mm<br>6 cts | 11.1 mm<br>5 cts | 10.3 mm<br>4 cts |
| 9.85 mm<br>3½ cts | 9,35 mm<br>3 cts | 8.8 mm<br>2½ cts | 8.5 mm<br>2¼ cts |

| | | | | |
|---|---|---|---|---|
| 8.2 mm<br>2 cts | 8.0 mm<br>1⅞ cts | 7.8 mm<br>1¾ cts | 7.6 mm<br>1⅝ cts | 7.4 mm<br>1½ cts |

| | | | | | |
|---|---|---|---|---|---|
| 7.2 mm<br>1⅜ cts | 7 mm<br>1¼ cts | 6.8 mm<br>1⅛ cts | 6.5 mm<br>1 ct | 6.2 mm<br>⅞ ct | 5.9 mm<br>¾ ct |
| 5.55 mm<br>⅝ ct | 5.15 mm<br>½ ct | 4.68 mm<br>⅜ ct | 4.1 mm<br>¼ ct | 3.25 mm<br>⅛ ct | 2.58 mm<br>¹⁄₁₆ ct |

Diameters of *round brilliant-cut* diamonds and their corresponding carat weight. GIA developed these approximations on the assumption that the proportions are good.

96

In discussing carat weight here, I pertain to the weight of one diamond. The weight of one diamond should not be confused with the total carat weight (TW) of more than one small diamond of equivalent weight, which are called *melees*. For example, the price of a 1-carat diamond solitaire ring is not the same as the price of a 1-carat TW 12-diamond wedding ring even if the diamonds are of the same quality. The price of the single 1 ct stone is very much higher that the price of the 12 diamonds 1 ct TW. This is because the supply of larger diamonds is limited than the supply of melees.

Melees are small diamonds from 0.00 0.45 points that are used to accentuate or surround a center stone on a piece of jewelry. They are also used to accentuate watch designs. The prices of melees are considerably lower than the large stones although they are also meticulously facetted to bring out the brilliance of each stone. A melee weighs up to .45 of a carat.

The ratio of a gemstone's density to the density of water is called *specific gravity*. It is because of specific gravity that a 1 ct ruby, which is more dense and heavier than diamond, is smaller than a 1 ct diamond. Diamond, on the other hand is more dense or heavier than turquoise such that a 1 ct diamond is smaller than a 1 ct turquoise. It is not safe to approximate the carat weight of your diamond based on the size and carat weight of other gemstones. They simply are not the same.

# Part III

## *Diamond Gem Stratagems*

### (Diamond Impostors and Diamond Make-Overs)

# 10 *Simulants and Synthetic Diamonds*

## *--- Diamond Look-Alikes*

Through the centuries, diamonds have always been the subject of awe and intrigue. Precious, valuable and mystical, the pellucid yet fiery diamond is nature's gift to man, a gift that he has designed to be more brilliant, more beautiful and more desirable. Its rarity contributed to this desirability and, for this reason, the diamond was once an item only for the royalty and, later, also for the rich, the mighty and the powerful. It was as if owning a diamond was a privilege that only the very few could enjoy. It was cherished as a talisman, a spellcaster, a charm for luck and good fortune

Modern times and empirical studies have somehow diminished the magical lore that encircled the diamond. Man's innate curiosity broke the mysticism. He also broke down a tradition of the ages. He can own a diamond himself ---- if only he can afford the exorbitant price. If not, he can own something that looks like a diamond. Why not? And to the diamond merchant, why not make more money out of selling an answer to a dream? Something that looks like a diamond but costs a lot less.

Imitation diamonds, called *simulants*, have been the bane of the industry. Euphemistically called diamond alternatives, they have fooled even the erudite diamond experts. A lot of people have been deceived and a lot more will be mislead because many do not know about simulants and how sophisticated they have become. The following are the commonly used diamond simulants:

## *Cubic Zirconia (CZ)*

Cubic Zirconia is a natural mineral found in igneous and sedimentary rocks. When properly cut and facetted, CZ looks like a diamond but does not possess the properties of a diamond. It merely looks like a diamond. To differentiate a diamond from a cubic zirconia, note the following:

- cubic zirconia displays more rainbow colors than diamond when exposed to a light source, especially under the sun;
- CZ is not as hard as diamond and will eventually become dull and worn;
- CZ has a higher density and is heavier than diamond of the same size;
- a diamond of the same size as a CZ will sink more slowly in heavy liquids.
- Inexpensive

## *Glass*

Rhinestones were originally made at Strasbourg (on the Rhine). It is a man-made gem that is bright and colorless made of hard glass cut in imitation of diamond. It would be helpful to note that glass (or rhinestone) has the following characteristics:

- brittle and easily chips off;
- the presence of gas bubbles is evident even to the naked eye;
- rounded facet angles and edges in comparison to diamond whose facets are sharp and defined;
- The absence of any inclusion except for the gas bubbles;
- Light will shine through glass. There is no light absorption whereas diamond will absorb and refract light;
- foil backed to reflect light and minimize dullness.
- Very, very cheap

## *Synthetic Spinel*

Synthetic Spinel is a man-made crystal that comes in a wide range of colors. Colorless spinel is used to imitate diamond. To differentiate from diamond, synthetic spinel has the following characteristics:

- less lustrous and with very limited dispersion;
- in polarized light, there is blurred, crosshatched appearance;
- presence of minute gas bubbles.
- Cheap

### Synthetic Rutile

This was widely used as a diamond imitation in the U.S. between 1940 and 1950. This man-made gem used to be manufactured in appreciable quantities during the 1950s but production now is very limited. Its characteristics are:

- very strong luster;
- slightly cloudy rather than perfectly transparent;
- facet edges are not sharp because of low hardness
- it feels slippery to the touch.
- cost is higher than cz or YAG

## Synthetic Strontium Titanate

This is wholly artificial and has no natural counterpart. It used to be marketed in 1955 as the first-rate imitation of diamond. Rendered obsolete after a few years because of the introduction of better diamond imitations with better hardness. Its characteristics are:

- low hardness;
- somewhat brittle;
- facet edges are not sharp and easily damaged;
- eventually displays a worn appearance;
- highly iridescent under strong light;
- perfectly colorless under diffused light;
- feels slippery to the touch.
- cost is higher than cz or YAG

## YAG (Yttrium Aluminium Garnet)

This is also wholly an artificial product with no known natural counterpart. This was the chief substitute for diamond in the 1960s. Its characteristics are:

- hard, not brittle;
- sharply defined facet edges;
- low dispersion, looks lifeless;

105

- highly transparent, you can see through the stone.

- Inexpensive

### *Synthetic Diamonds*

It has been discovered that diamonds are not for body adornment alone. The discovery that diamond is a highly effective and efficient industrial material gave rise to the manufacture of industrial diamonds. The discovery of manufacturing diamonds was more out of necessity to allay fears and apprehension that there would not be enough supply of natural industrial diamonds for the wider use. It was also an endeavor to bring the prices down in the long run. It did not take long before manufactured diamonds, called *created* or *lab-grown* by its marketers and promoters, found its way to the jewelry industry.

Synthetic diamonds are diamonds that are created under the same situation of extreme heat and pressure as natural diamonds ---- but in a laboratory. A synthetic diamond has the same crystalline structure and the same properties as that of a natural diamond. The production of a synthetic diamond is still quite costly but it is projected that as technology improves, the cost of production will eventually decrease. This should put the market price of synthetic diamonds to very affordable levels.

How to differentiate a synthetic diamond from a natural diamond is the problem that consumers will have to face. Synthetic diamonds do have distinct characteristics and they are:

- ultraviolet fluorescence is stronger and uneven;
- phosphorescence that makes the stone glow after the light source is turned off;
- the presence of metallic inclusions which makes the stone attracted to magnets.
- Costs about 65% less than natural diamonds.

### Moissanite

Moissanite, or C3, is a diamond alternative that has caused some ripples in the diamond industry. C3 is one diamond look-alike that has passed most diamond testers! Produced by a manufacturing company based in North Carolina, C3 is not a synthetic diamond but a diamond simulant. To differentiate C3 from a natural diamond, the following are its characteristics:

- has a higher refractive index than the diamond;
- has a higher dispersion than diamond;

107

- lower density than diamond;
- will float in pure methylene iodide while diamond will sink.

Simulants and synthetic diamonds will always be there for as long as the diamond remains a status symbol of wealth and luxury. Many more will be created to imitate the diamond to cash in on the demand and the price of this magnificent stone. The positive effect of simulant and synthetic diamonds on the consumers is that:

1. the average consumer can now afford to buy an alternative to a diamond ---- and it is not glass;
2. owners of natural diamonds will appreciate their diamonds all the more because natural is always better.

# 11 *Investing On Diamonds For Profit And Pleasure*

I have always emphasized from the beginning of the book that the diamond is an asset and as an asset, it can be turned into liquid cash anytime we want to, anytime that it is necessary. The portability of the diamond makes this possible. Real estate is an asset, and so are cars, stocks and bonds. But in case of exigencies, these assets are hard to sell at a moment's notice. Real estate is difficult to liquidate. It will take weeks, perhaps months in listing, before a property can be sold. Cars and automobiles depreciate from the moment that they leave the dealership and the papers are transferred to your name. Sell your car the following day and it automatically becomes a second-hand car! Not with diamonds. A high quality diamond bought at the right price will not depreciate. The only way that its resale price will go is up or, at least, just at the price that it was bought but seldom down.

When one buys a diamond, the intention is usually not just as an adornment, but also for its resale value ---- something like having money in the bank as a financial security. If the objective in buying a diamond is only for the sheer pleasure of owning one, an

SI grade level may be sufficient. However, if the objective is two-pronged --- to own and to resell at a much later date, it is prudent to buy a better quality stone, a stone with a grade level that is higher than SI.

It is not easy buying a diamond for investment only because the enjoyment of owning a diamond is minimized. Also, there is a natural tendency to be always on the lookout for the market price to go up. It is more an eagerness to see that the value of the asset is going up and the money is growing someplace. Perhaps this is a psychological pleasure and as pleasant an experience as the sense of ownership and possession.

Whatever is the reason for the purchase of a diamond, it is advisable to be informed of the commodity first. Putting money in the purchase of something valuable must not be based on trust alone. Know what you are buying. Read more on diamonds and learn about what makes the diamond valuable. Read on what devaluates it. There is absolutely nothing wrong in being a well-informed buyer. No matter how credible or reputable the jeweler is, the diamond must be worth the money being spent on it. For instance, a good resale value is possible provided that the diamond is really of high quality and grade, that it was a good buy based on the result of your comparison of the prices of other stores/dealers and you have set up a liquidation plan in advance. Setting up a liquidation plan merely means that you have studied the market and know exactly where to sell your diamond at the time that you want to sell it. This way, you are not at the mercy of your buyer when you need the liquid cash the most.

Invest on a minimum of 1 ct round brilliant cut, SI or better, color grade H or higher. Do not invest on fancy cuts. Set your sights instead on commercial rounds because this has a wider market and is always on demand.

Why diamonds? Why invest on diamonds? Other than the joy and pleasure of possessing something that was once only for the royalty and they provide the security of money without the insecurity of inflation. Money is subject to the various elements that move the economy and gets affected by changes. Diamond is not subject to economic change. Its portability makes it an excellent source of funds after wars, catastrophes and when you are in flight from political chaos.

Investing on diamonds may be worth your while and your money. Be sure to learn about diamonds first. Even doing so is worth your while.

# 12
*Consumer Tips*

In looking for a good buy, consider the following places. When you go to look at a diamond, be sure to bear in mind that you do not have to buy . Do not be pressured into buying or committing yourself to buy a stone whose quality you are not sure.

## *Pawnshops*

Most pawnshops sell their diamonds or diamond jewelry at a very reasonable price after the date of redemption. This is because pawnshops want to have their money back plus interest to be able to lend out again. Pawnshop capital has to move and in order to do so, they must sell their inventories quickly.

## *Classified Ads*

Some advertisers in the Classified Ads who are selling their diamond jewelry are those who recently broke up with their partners or recently divorced. They want to quickly get rid of anything that would remind them of the other party. It would be good to look into this but do not forget though that this reason can also be used by a scam artist who is out to sell a fake diamond. Contact the advertiser and arrange to meet in a bank where there are security guards. If the jewelry is real and of good quality, you are both in a neutral and safe place.

## Estate Sales

Old mine cuts and old European cuts are usually found in estate sales and may be bought at very reasonable prices especially if the families only want to liquidate some personal property.

## Street Hawkers

Never buy your diamonds from the street. It is not logically credible that anyone would be hawking real diamonds out in the streets. It is more likely that you will be duped into buying a rhinestone.

## "We buy gold and diamonds"

Be extra careful of buying diamonds from places where you see this sign. Chances are, they will sell you a cz or a synthetic diamond.

Before I finally end this book, there is a word of advice that I wish to share. In buying a diamond, or anything for that matter, never forget that a great part of the sales transaction is persuasion. What is important in a sales transaction is that one party should be able to sell to the other party. It is very seldom that you find a jeweler who would be happy just to talk to you about gems in this transaction. Most will persuade you into buying. This is the reason why I find it most important to impart a few nuggets of thought and my experience in the trade so that others may learn from what I know. It is difficult to find somebody who will disclose everything to the buyer about the imperfections of something as beautiful as the sparkling diamond on the counter. He will highlight its beauty and try to omit its possible lopsidedness or the shallowness of its pavilion. It is as if all its scintillation comes from its fiery depth unmarred by an undisclosed glass filler. Do not be blinded and listen less to the persuasion and look more into the diamond. After all, there are good reasons why you should know what you are buying. And the foremost reason is because it is your hard-earned cash that will pay for that stone. Furthermore, do not forget that you can look through a loupe or a microscope. Know the diamond --- up close and personal.

# APPENDICES

# APPENDIX A

## Diamond Consumer's Bill of Rights

*Department of Consumer Affairs Tips for Jewelry
and Loose Diamond Buyers*

New consumer protection regulations have been proposed by the New York City Department of Consumer Affairs. We hope the advice and tips from the *Consumer Bill of Rights* outlined by the Consumer Affairs Commissioner, Jules Polonetsky, will be adopted as a guideline for other cities and states to protect jewelry and loose diamond buyers. This author joins with Commissioner Polonetsky to urge jewelers to disseminate the DCA Jewelry Buyer's Bill of Rights so that consumers "can arm themselves with the most important tool needed to be a successful shopper – an education."

As a protection against "bogus bargains," the phrase coined by Commissioner Polonetsky, the Department of Consumer Affairs (DCA) released the *"Jewelry Buyer's Bill of Rights"*:

- ◆ You have the right to a receipt for all purchases over $20 which includes the price, the tax amount and the legal name of the seller.

- ◆ You have the right to a detailed receipt for purchases over $75 which includes the

116

above information as well as a description of the article and its composition. In the case of diamonds, a receipt must also include accurate diamond grading and carat weight information.

♦ You have the right to know the jeweler's refund and exchange policy.

♦ You have the right to information disclosing any treatments or enhancements to the stone you purchase.

♦ You have the right to pay the currently advertised price. A jeweler must live up to the price or discount advertised on a flyer or in the newspaper.

♦ We recommend you avoid shopping at stores that employ hawkers who stand on the sidewalk and use high-pressure tactics to draw you into their stores.

♦ In New York City, you have the right to file a complaint with the DCA if you have a dispute with a jeweler.

The proposed New York City regulations would target businesses who "inflate the price of merchandise in order to make exaggerated sales claims." One of the culprits cited in the Department's inspection sweep of the New York City businesses was a major department store. DCA inspectors were shown "a pair of plain, 14-karat gold earrings" marked 50% off, with an additional 15% off the original price of $300. But when the inspectors had the earrings appraised by jewelry specialist, they were told the fair market value was $127.50. Once the numbers have been crunched, one finds that the "sale" price was exactly what the original price should have been.

Now some may ask, if the business running the "inflate and mark-down scam" does eventually get down to the price item ought to be, why should there be any regulations? The answer affects all those in the jewelry trade. Though a customer attracted by the false 50% off advertisements may be fooled, retailers, who are more scrupulous in their advertising, are at a serious disadvantage. Even though they may be offering competitive prices, they're not making outlandish sale claims," said Commissioner Polonetsky. It is in no ones best interest to cheat the purchasing public.

Commissioner Polonetsky said, "I applaud the 47th Street Business Improvement District (BID) for proactively seeking to educate their customers by urging their merchants to post the DCA jewelry Buyers Bill of Rights in their stores." The Commissioner also offered consumer tips for purchasing diamond jewelry:

> Buy from a trusted firm.
>
> Have the jewelry appraised by an independent party.

Ask about "Fracture Filled" and other treatments.

Look for gold trademarks and karat weight.

Don't be dazzled by discounts.

# APPENDIX B

## *Guide to the Price Guide*

---
### Color Grading Scale
---

| D | E | F | G | H | I | J | K | L | M |
|---|---|---|---|---|---|---|---|---|---|
| *Colorless* | | | *Near colorless* | | | | *Faint Yellow* | | |

---
### Clarity Grading Scale
---

| IF | VVS-1 | VVS-2 | VS-1 | VS-2 | SI-1 | SI-2 | SI-3 | I-1 | I-2 | I-3 |
|----|-------|-------|------|------|------|------|------|-----|-----|-----|
| Flawless | Very very slight inclusions | | Very slight inclusions | | Slight Inclusions | | | Imperfect | | |

| Seen only w/ a binocular microscope | Seen through a loupe of 10x magnification |
|---|---|

### Clarity Grading Scale Description

IF: Internally Flawless    No inclusions and only significant surface blemishes seen through a binocular microscope.

120

| VVS1 and VVS2: Very, Very Slight Inclusions | Minute inclusions that are difficult to see unless through a binocular microscope |
| --- | --- |
| VS1 and VS2: Very Slight Inclusions | Minor inclusions ranging from difficult to somewhat easy to see face up, under 10x magnification. |
| SI1 and SI2: Slight Inclusions | Noticeable inclusions that are easy (SI1) or very easy (SI2) to see under 10x magnification. Eye-clean, face up, to the naked eye. |
| I1, I2, and I3: Imperfect | Obvious inclusions that are usually visible, face up, to the naked eye. Distinctions are based on durability, transparency and brilliance. |

How to compute diamond price based on the *Price Guide*.

1. Determine the diamond shape or cut and turn to that page on the Price Guide.

2. Color is the first left column of the chart in conjunction to clarity grading at the top row, which gives the cost per carat. All figures are in US $.

3. Price from intersection of Color/Clarity X Carat Weight = Total Price.

    For example:
        Color Grade = I
        Clarity = VS1
        Weight = 3.07 carats
        Shape: Round Brilliant Cut
        $9,400 per carat X 3.07 carats = $28,858.00

How to compute with discounted price.

Every buyer has the right to negotiate for a discount from the seller. For example, the negotiated discount is 25%:
If total price = $28,858.00 X 25% = $7,214.50

        $28,858.00 - $7,213.50 = $21,644.50

# *Price Guide*

SHAPE: ROUND               CARAT: ¼ or .25

| | | | | .23 to .29 ct | | | | |
|---|---|---|---|---|---|---|---|---|
| | IF - VVS | VS | SI1 | SI2 | SI3 | I1 | I2 | I3 |
| D | 2100 | 1600 | 1250 | 1100 | 960 | 860 | 770 | 510 |
| E | 2100 | 1600 | 1250 | 1100 | 960 | 860 | 770 | 510 |
| F | 2100 | 1600 | 1250 | 1100 | 960 | 860 | 770 | 510 |
| G | 1600 | 1450 | 1150 | 1050 | 930 | 830 | 750 | 490 |
| H | 1600 | 1450 | 1150 | 1050 | 930 | 830 | 750 | 490 |
| I | 1300 | 1200 | 1050 | 980 | 860 | 780 | 650 | 430 |
| J | 1300 | 1200 | 1050 | 980 | 860 | 780 | 650 | 430 |
| K | 1100 | 1000 | 950 | 900 | 800 | 750 | 600 | 380 |
| L | 1100 | 1000 | 950 | 900 | 800 | 750 | 600 | 380 |
| M | 900 | 850 | 800 | 700 | 650 | 600 | 500 | 350 |

SHAPE: EMERALD       CARAT: ¼ or .25

| | | | | .23 to .29 ct | | | | |
|---|---|---|---|---|---|---|---|---|
| | IF - VVS | VS | SI1 | SI2 | SI3 | I1 | I2 | I3 |
| D | 1430 | 1240 | 950 | 860 | 760 | 690 | 570 | 430 |
| E | 1430 | 1240 | 950 | 860 | 760 | 690 | 570 | 430 |
| F | 1430 | 1240 | 950 | 860 | 760 | 690 | 570 | 430 |
| G | 1240 | 1000 | 860 | 760 | 710 | 670 | 520 | 380 |
| H | 1240 | 1000 | 860 | 760 | 710 | 670 | 520 | 380 |
| I | 1000 | 900 | 790 | 710 | 680 | 640 | 480 | 330 |
| J | 1000 | 900 | 790 | 710 | 680 | 640 | 480 | 330 |
| K | 860 | 810 | 710 | 630 | 600 | 570 | 430 | 290 |
| L | 860 | 810 | 710 | 630 | 600 | 570 | 430 | 290 |
| M | 710 | 620 | 520 | 480 | 440 | 400 | 350 | 250 |

Please use these figures only as a point of comparison.
These prices are the author's opinion. B.J. Tadena
assumes no liability and makes no guarantees as to the
accuracy of these charts. For updated and accurate industry
price, refer to the Rapaport Diamond Report.

# *Price Guide*

SHAPE: PEAR                 CARAT: ¼ or .25

| | .23 to .29 ct | | | | | | | |
|---|---|---|---|---|---|---|---|---|
| | IF - VVS | VS | SI1 | SI2 | SI3 | I1 | I2 | I3 |
| D | 1500 | 1300 | 1000 | 900 | 800 | 730 | 600 | 450 |
| E | 1500 | 1300 | 1000 | 900 | 800 | 730 | 600 | 450 |
| F | 1500 | 1300 | 1000 | 900 | 800 | 730 | 600 | 450 |
| G | 1300 | 1050 | 900 | 800 | 750 | 710 | 550 | 400 |
| H | 1300 | 1050 | 900 | 800 | 750 | 710 | 550 | 400 |
| I | 1050 | 950 | 830 | 750 | 720 | 670 | 500 | 350 |
| J | 1050 | 950 | 830 | 750 | 720 | 670 | 500 | 350 |
| K | 900 | 850 | 750 | 660 | 630 | 600 | 450 | 300 |
| L | 900 | 850 | 750 | 660 | 630 | 600 | 450 | 300 |
| M | 750 | 650 | 550 | 500 | 460 | 420 | 370 | 260 |

SHAPE: MARQUISE       CARAT: ¼ or .25

| | .23 to .29 ct | | | | | | | |
|---|---|---|---|---|---|---|---|---|
| | IF - VVS | VS | SI1 | SI2 | SI3 | I1 | I2 | I3 |
| D | 1600 | 1400 | 1100 | 1000 | 900 | 830 | 690 | 520 |
| E | 1600 | 1400 | 1100 | 1000 | 900 | 830 | 690 | 520 |
| F | 1600 | 1400 | 1100 | 1000 | 900 | 830 | 690 | 520 |
| G | 1400 | 1150 | 1000 | 900 | 850 | 810 | 630 | 460 |
| H | 1400 | 1150 | 1000 | 900 | 850 | 810 | 630 | 460 |
| I | 1150 | 1050 | 930 | 850 | 820 | 770 | 580 | 400 |
| J | 1150 | 1050 | 930 | 850 | 820 | 770 | 580 | 400 |
| K | 1000 | 950 | 850 | 760 | 720 | 690 | 520 | 350 |
| L | 1000 | 950 | 850 | 760 | 720 | 690 | 520 | 350 |
| M | 850 | 750 | 630 | 580 | 530 | 480 | 430 | 300 |

Please use these figures only as a point of comparison.
These prices are the author's opinion. B.J. Tadena
assumes no liability and makes no guarantees as to the
accuracy of these charts. For updated and accurate industry
price, refer to the Rapaport Diamond Report.

# *Price Guide*

SHAPE: ROUND          CARAT: ½ or .5

| | | | | | .50 to .69 ct | | | | | | |
|---|---|---|---|---|---|---|---|---|---|---|---|
| | IF | VVS1 | VVS2 | VS1 | VS2 | S11 | S12 | S13 | I1 | I2 | I3 |
| D | 8100 | 6600 | 6000 | 5000 | 4100 | 3500 | 2800 | 2500 | 2100 | 1500 | 1100 |
| E | 6600 | 6100 | 5200 | 4700 | 4000 | 3400 | 2700 | 2400 | 2000 | 1400 | 1000 |
| F | 6100 | 5300 | 4700 | 4400 | 3800 | 3200 | 2600 | 2300 | 1900 | 1300 | 1000 |
| G | 5300 | 4700 | 4300 | 4100 | 3600 | 3000 | 2500 | 2200 | 1800 | 1300 | 900 |
| H | 4500 | 4100 | 3700 | 3500 | 3100 | 2800 | 2300 | 2000 | 1700 | 1200 | 900 |
| I | 3600 | 3300 | 3100 | 2800 | 2600 | 2400 | 2200 | 1900 | 1600 | 1200 | 900 |
| J | 3000 | 2800 | 2600 | 2500 | 2400 | 2300 | 2100 | 1800 | 1500 | 1200 | 800 |
| K | 2400 | 2300 | 2200 | 2100 | 2000 | 1900 | 1700 | 1600 | 1400 | 1100 | 800 |
| L | 2300 | 2200 | 2100 | 2000 | 1900 | 1800 | 1600 | 1400 | 1100 | 1000 | 700 |
| M | 2000 | 1900 | 1800 | 1700 | 1600 | 1500 | 1400 | 1200 | 1000 | 900 | 600 |

EMERALD          CARAT: ½ or .5

| | | | | | .50 to .69 ct | | | | | | |
|---|---|---|---|---|---|---|---|---|---|---|---|
| | IF | VVS1 | VVS2 | VS1 | VS2 | S11 | S12 | S13 | I1 | I2 | I3 |
| D | 5000 | 4400 | 4100 | 3600 | 3200 | 2800 | 2400 | 2100 | 1800 | 1400 | 1100 |
| E | 4400 | 4100 | 3600 | 3200 | 2900 | 2700 | 2300 | 2000 | 1700 | 1300 | 1000 |
| F | 4000 | 3600 | 3200 | 2900 | 2800 | 2600 | 2200 | 1900 | 1600 | 1200 | 1000 |
| G | 3500 | 3200 | 2900 | 2800 | 2600 | 2400 | 2100 | 1800 | 1500 | 1200 | 900 |
| H | 3100 | 2900 | 2700 | 2600 | 2400 | 2200 | 2000 | 1700 | 1400 | 1100 | 900 |
| I | 2800 | 2500 | 2400 | 2300 | 2200 | 2100 | 1900 | 1600 | 1400 | 1000 | 800 |
| J | 2300 | 2200 | 2100 | 2000 | 1900 | 1800 | 1600 | 1400 | 1300 | 900 | 800 |
| K | 1800 | 1700 | 1700 | 1600 | 1600 | 1500 | 1400 | 1300 | 1100 | 900 | 700 |
| L | 1500 | 1400 | 1400 | 1300 | 1300 | 1200 | 1100 | 1000 | 900 | 800 | 700 |
| M | 1300 | 1300 | 1300 | 1200 | 1200 | 1100 | 1000 | 900 | 800 | 700 | 600 |

Please use these figures only as a point of comparison.
These prices are the author's opinion.  B.J. Tadena
assumes no liability and makes no guarantees as to the
accuracy of these charts. For updated and accurate industry
price, refer to the Rapaport Diamond Report.

# *Price Guide*

PEAR                           CARAT: ½ or .5

| | | | | | .50 to .69 ct | | | | | | |
|---|---|---|---|---|---|---|---|---|---|---|---|
| | IF | VVS1 | VVS2 | VS1 | VS2 | S11 | S12 | S13 | I1 | I2 | I3 |
| D | 5700 | 5000 | 4600 | 4100 | 3600 | 3100 | 2700 | 2400 | 2000 | 1500 | 1100 |
| E | 5000 | 4600 | 4100 | 3600 | 3300 | 3000 | 2600 | 2300 | 1900 | 1400 | 1000 |
| F | 4600 | 4100 | 3600 | 3300 | 3100 | 2900 | 2500 | 2200 | 1800 | 1300 | 1000 |
| G | 4100 | 3600 | 3300 | 3100 | 2900 | 2700 | 2400 | 2100 | 1700 | 1300 | 900 |
| H | 3600 | 3300 | 3100 | 2900 | 2700 | 2500 | 2300 | 2000 | 1600 | 1200 | 900 |
| I | 3200 | 2900 | 2800 | 2600 | 2500 | 2400 | 2200 | 1900 | 1500 | 1200 | 800 |
| J | 2600 | 2500 | 2400 | 2300 | 2200 | 2100 | 1900 | 1700 | 1400 | 1100 | 800 |
| K | 2000 | 1900 | 1900 | 1800 | 1800 | 1700 | 1600 | 1500 | 1200 | 1000 | 700 |
| L | 1700 | 1600 | 1600 | 1500 | 1500 | 1400 | 1300 | 1200 | 900 | 800 | 700 |
| M | 1400 | 1400 | 1400 | 1300 | 1300 | 1200 | 1100 | 1000 | 800 | 700 | 600 |

MARQUISE                       CARAT: ½ or .50

| | | | | | .50 to .69 ct | | | | | | |
|---|---|---|---|---|---|---|---|---|---|---|---|
| | IF | VVS1 | VVS2 | VS1 | VS2 | S11 | S12 | S13 | I1 | I2 | I3 |
| D | 5700 | 5000 | 4600 | 4100 | 3600 | 3100 | 2700 | 2400 | 2000 | 1500 | 1100 |
| E | 5000 | 4600 | 4100 | 3700 | 3400 | 3100 | 2600 | 2300 | 1900 | 1400 | 1000 |
| F | 4600 | 4100 | 3600 | 3400 | 3200 | 3000 | 2500 | 2200 | 1800 | 1300 | 1000 |
| G | 4100 | 3600 | 3300 | 3200 | 3000 | 2800 | 2400 | 2100 | 1700 | 1300 | 900 |
| H | 3600 | 3300 | 3100 | 3000 | 2800 | 2600 | 2300 | 2000 | 1600 | 1200 | 900 |
| I | 3200 | 2900 | 2800 | 2700 | 2600 | 2500 | 2200 | 1900 | 1500 | 1200 | 800 |
| J | 2600 | 2500 | 2400 | 2300 | 2200 | 2000 | 1900 | 1800 | 1400 | 1100 | 800 |
| K | 2000 | 1900 | 1900 | 1800 | 1800 | 1700 | 1600 | 1500 | 1200 | 1000 | 700 |
| L | 1700 | 1600 | 1600 | 1500 | 1500 | 1400 | 1300 | 1200 | 900 | 800 | 700 |
| M | 1500 | 1400 | 1400 | 1300 | 1300 | 1200 | 1100 | 1000 | 800 | 700 | 600 |

Please use these figures only as a point of comparison.
These prices are the author's opinion. B.J. Tadena
assumes no liability and makes no guarantees as to the
accuracy of these charts. For updated and accurate industry
price, refer to the Rapaport Diamond Report.

# *Price Guide*

SHAPE: ROUND                 CARAT: ¾ or .75

| | | | | | | .70 to .89 ct | | | | | |
|---|---|---|---|---|---|---|---|---|---|---|---|
| | IF | VVS1 | VVS2 | VS1 | VS2 | S11 | S12 | S13 | I1 | I2 | I3 |
| D | 8800 | 7000 | 6300 | 5500 | 4900 | 4500 | 4000 | 3400 | 2700 | 1800 | 1200 |
| E | 7000 | 6500 | 5600 | 5100 | 4700 | 4400 | 3900 | 3200 | 2600 | 1800 | 1100 |
| F | 6400 | 5700 | 5100 | 4800 | 4500 | 4300 | 3800 | 3100 | 2600 | 1700 | 1100 |
| G | 5600 | 5100 | 4800 | 4500 | 4300 | 4000 | 3600 | 3000 | 2500 | 1700 | 1000 |
| II | 5000 | 4600 | 4400 | 4200 | 4000 | 3700 | 3400 | 2800 | 2400 | 1600 | 1000 |
| I | 4300 | 4100 | 3900 | 3700 | 3600 | 3400 | 3000 | 2600 | 2300 | 1500 | 1000 |
| J | 3700 | 3600 | 3500 | 3300 | 3100 | 2900 | 2700 | 2300 | 2200 | 1400 | 900 |
| K | 3300 | 3200 | 3100 | 2900 | 2700 | 2500 | 2300 | 2000 | 1800 | 1300 | 900 |
| L | 2700 | 2600 | 2500 | 2400 | 2300 | 2200 | 2000 | 1600 | 1300 | 1100 | 800 |
| M | 2500 | 2400 | 2300 | 2200 | 2100 | 2000 | 1800 | 1500 | 1200 | 1000 | 700 |

EMERALD                       CARAT: ¾ or .75

| | | | | | | .70 to .89 ct | | | | | |
|---|---|---|---|---|---|---|---|---|---|---|---|
| | IF | VVS1 | VVS2 | VS1 | VS2 | S11 | S12 | S13 | I1 | I2 | I3 |
| D | 6700 | 5300 | 5000 | 4700 | 4300 | 3900 | 3300 | 2700 | 2200 | 1500 | 1100 |
| E | 5300 | 5000 | 4700 | 4500 | 4200 | 3800 | 3200 | 2600 | 2100 | 1500 | 1100 |
| F | 4900 | 4600 | 4400 | 4300 | 4100 | 3700 | 3100 | 2500 | 2000 | 1400 | 1000 |
| G | 4500 | 4400 | 4200 | 4100 | 4000 | 3500 | 3000 | 2400 | 1900 | 1400 | 1000 |
| H | 4100 | 4000 | 3900 | 3800 | 3700 | 3300 | 2800 | 2300 | 1800 | 1400 | 900 |
| I | 3600 | 3500 | 3400 | 3300 | 3300 | 3000 | 2400 | 2100 | 1700 | 1300 | 900 |
| J | 3200 | 3100 | 3000 | 2900 | 2800 | 2500 | 2200 | 1800 | 1500 | 1200 | 800 |
| K | 2700 | 2600 | 2500 | 2400 | 2300 | 2100 | 1900 | 1700 | 1400 | 1100 | 800 |
| L | 2200 | 2100 | 2000 | 1900 | 1800 | 1700 | 1600 | 1400 | 1100 | 1000 | 700 |
| M | 1600 | 1600 | 1600 | 1500 | 1500 | 1400 | 1300 | 1200 | 900 | 800 | 600 |

Please use these figures only as a point of comparison.
These prices are the author's opinion. B.J. Tadena
assumes no liability and makes no guarantees as to the
accuracy of these charts. For updated and accurate industry
price, refer to the Rapaport Diamond Report.

# *Price Guide*

PEAR  CARAT: ¾ or .75

| | IF | VVS1 | VVS2 | VS1 | VS2 | S11 | S12 | S13 | I1 | I2 | I3 |
|---|---|---|---|---|---|---|---|---|---|---|---|
| | | | | .70 to .89 ct | | | | | | | |
| D | 7400 | 5900 | 5500 | 5100 | 4700 | 4300 | 3700 | 3100 | 2400 | 1700 | 1200 |
| E | 5900 | 5500 | 5100 | 4900 | 4600 | 4200 | 3600 | 3000 | 2300 | 1700 | 1100 |
| F | 5500 | 5100 | 4900 | 4700 | 4500 | 4100 | 3500 | 2900 | 2200 | 1600 | 1100 |
| G | 5100 | 4900 | 4700 | 4500 | 4300 | 3900 | 3400 | 2800 | 2100 | 1600 | 1000 |
| H | 4700 | 4500 | 4400 | 4200 | 4000 | 3700 | 3100 | 2600 | 2000 | 1500 | 1000 |
| I | 4100 | 4000 | 3900 | 3800 | 3600 | 3400 | 2800 | 2400 | 1900 | 1400 | 900 |
| J | 3500 | 3400 | 3300 | 3200 | 3100 | 2900 | 2500 | 2100 | 1700 | 1300 | 900 |
| K | 2900 | 2800 | 2700 | 2600 | 2500 | 2300 | 2100 | 1900 | 1500 | 1200 | 800 |
| L | 2400 | 2300 | 2200 | 2100 | 2000 | 1900 | 1800 | 1600 | 1200 | 1000 | 800 |
| M | 1700 | 1700 | 1700 | 1600 | 1600 | 1500 | 1400 | 1300 | 900 | 800 | 700 |

MARQUISE  CARAT: ¾ or .75

| | IF | VVS1 | VVS2 | VS1 | VS2 | S11 | S12 | S13 | I1 | I2 | I3 |
|---|---|---|---|---|---|---|---|---|---|---|---|
| | | | | .70 to .89 ct | | | | | | | |
| D | 7500 | 6100 | 5800 | 5400 | 5000 | 4600 | 3900 | 3300 | 2500 | 1800 | 1200 |
| E | 6000 | 5700 | 5400 | 5100 | 4900 | 4500 | 3800 | 3200 | 2400 | 1800 | 1200 |
| F | 5600 | 5300 | 5100 | 4900 | 4800 | 4400 | 3700 | 3000 | 2300 | 1700 | 1100 |
| G | 5200 | 5100 | 4900 | 4700 | 4600 | 4200 | 3600 | 2900 | 2200 | 1700 | 1000 |
| H | 4800 | 4700 | 4600 | 4400 | 4200 | 3900 | 3300 | 2800 | 2100 | 1600 | 1000 |
| I | 4200 | 4100 | 4000 | 3900 | 3700 | 3500 | 3000 | 2600 | 2000 | 1500 | 900 |
| J | 3600 | 3500 | 3400 | 3300 | 3200 | 3000 | 2600 | 2200 | 1800 | 1400 | 900 |
| K | 3000 | 2900 | 2800 | 2700 | 2600 | 2400 | 2200 | 2000 | 1600 | 1300 | 800 |
| L | 2500 | 2400 | 2300 | 2200 | 2100 | 2000 | 1900 | 1600 | 1200 | 1000 | 700 |
| M | 1800 | 1700 | 1700 | 1600 | 1600 | 1500 | 1400 | 1300 | 900 | 800 | 600 |

Please use these figures only as a point of comparison.
These prices are the author's opinion. B.J. Tadena
assumes no liability and makes no guarantees as to the
accuracy of these charts. For updated and accurate industry
price, refer to the Rapaport Diamond Report.

# Price Guide

SHAPE: ROUND          CARAT: 1.00

| | | | | | 1.00 to 1.49 ct | | | | | | |
|---|---|---|---|---|---|---|---|---|---|---|---|
| | IF | VVS1 | VVS2 | VS1 | VS2 | S11 | S12 | S13 | I1 | I2 | I3 |
| D | 16400 | 11100 | 9600 | 7800 | 6800 | 6000 | 5400 | 4300 | 3500 | 2400 | 1500 |
| E | 11100 | 9800 | 7900 | 7200 | 6600 | 5900 | 5300 | 4200 | 3400 | 2400 | 1400 |
| F | 9700 | 8000 | 7200 | 6900 | 6400 | 5800 | 5100 | 4100 | 3300 | 2300 | 1400 |
| G | 7900 | 7200 | 6800 | 6500 | 6100 | 5600 | 4900 | 3900 | 3200 | 2200 | 1300 |
| H | 6900 | 6600 | 6300 | 6000 | 5700 | 5300 | 4700 | 3800 | 3100 | 2100 | 1300 |
| I | 0100 | 5800 | 5500 | 5300 | 5000 | 4700 | 4200 | 3700 | 3000 | 1900 | 1200 |
| J | 5400 | 5200 | 5000 | 4800 | 4600 | 4200 | 3800 | 3300 | 2800 | 1800 | 1200 |
| K | 4900 | 4700 | 4600 | 4400 | 4100 | 3900 | 3500 | 3100 | 2600 | 1700 | 1100 |
| L | 4300 | 4200 | 4000 | 3800 | 3600 | 3400 | 3100 | 2800 | 2300 | 1600 | 1000 |
| M | 3500 | 3400 | 3300 | 3100 | 2900 | 2700 | 2500 | 2300 | 1900 | 1500 | 1000 |

EMERALD          CARAT: 1.00

| | | | | | 1.00 to 1.49 ct | | | | | | |
|---|---|---|---|---|---|---|---|---|---|---|---|
| | IF | VVS1 | VVS2 | VS1 | VS2 | S11 | S12 | S13 | I1 | I2 | I3 |
| D | 11200 | 7400 | 6500 | 6300 | 5900 | 5000 | 4300 | 3500 | 2800 | 2100 | 1200 |
| E | 7300 | 6500 | 6200 | 6000 | 5700 | 4800 | 4200 | 3400 | 2700 | 2000 | 1200 |
| F | 6400 | 6100 | 5900 | 5700 | 5400 | 4600 | 4100 | 3300 | 2600 | 2000 | 1100 |
| G | 5900 | 5800 | 5500 | 5400 | 5100 | 4400 | 3900 | 3200 | 2500 | 1900 | 1100 |
| H | 5500 | 5200 | 5000 | 4800 | 4500 | 4000 | 3600 | 3000 | 2400 | 1800 | 1000 |
| I | 4700 | 4600 | 4400 | 4200 | 4000 | 3700 | 3200 | 2800 | 2300 | 1700 | 1000 |
| J | 4100 | 3900 | 3700 | 3500 | 3300 | 3100 | 2800 | 2400 | 2100 | 1400 | 1000 |
| K | 3500 | 3400 | 3300 | 3200 | 3000 | 2900 | 2600 | 2200 | 2000 | 1300 | 1000 |
| L | 3000 | 2900 | 2800 | 2700 | 2500 | 2300 | 2100 | 1800 | 1600 | 1100 | 900 |
| M | 2500 | 2400 | 2300 | 2200 | 2100 | 1900 | 1700 | 1600 | 1300 | 1100 | 700 |

Please use these figures only as a point of comparison.
These prices are the author's opinion. B.J. Tadena
assumes no liability and makes no guarantees as to the
accuracy of these charts. For updated and accurate industry
price, refer to the Rapaport Diamond Report.

# *Price Guide*

PEAR             CARAT: 1.00

| | | | | | 1.00 to 1.49 ct | | | | | | |
|---|---|---|---|---|---|---|---|---|---|---|---|
| | IF | VVS1 | VVS2 | VS1 | VS2 | S11 | S12 | S13 | I1 | I2 | I3 |
| D | 12700 | 8200 | 7200 | 6800 | 6400 | 5500 | 4600 | 3900 | 3100 | 2300 | 1400 |
| E | 8200 | 7200 | 6800 | 6500 | 6200 | 5300 | 4500 | 3800 | 3000 | 2200 | 1300 |
| F | 7200 | 6800 | 6500 | 6200 | 5800 | 5100 | 4400 | 3700 | 2900 | 2200 | 1300 |
| G | 6700 | 6400 | 6100 | 5800 | 5500 | 4900 | 4300 | 3600 | 2800 | 2100 | 1200 |
| H | 6300 | 5900 | 5600 | 5300 | 5000 | 4600 | 4100 | 3400 | 2700 | 2000 | 1200 |
| I | 5400 | 5200 | 5000 | 4800 | 4500 | 4200 | 3700 | 3200 | 2600 | 1900 | 1100 |
| J | 4500 | 4300 | 4100 | 3900 | 3700 | 3500 | 3200 | 2700 | 2300 | 1600 | 1100 |
| K | 3800 | 3700 | 3600 | 3500 | 3300 | 3100 | 2800 | 2400 | 2100 | 1400 | 1000 |
| L | 3200 | 3100 | 3000 | 2900 | 2700 | 2500 | 2300 | 2000 | 1700 | 1200 | 900 |
| M | 2500 | 2500 | 2400 | 2300 | 2200 | 2000 | 1800 | 1700 | 1300 | 1100 | 800 |

MARQUISE           CARAT: 1.00

| | | | | | 1.00 to 1.49 ct | | | | | | |
|---|---|---|---|---|---|---|---|---|---|---|---|
| | IF | VVS1 | VVS2 | VS1 | VS2 | S11 | S12 | S13 | I1 | I2 | I3 |
| D | 12700 | 8200 | 7400 | 7100 | 6700 | 5800 | 4900 | 4100 | 3300 | 2400 | 1400 |
| E | 8200 | 7400 | 7100 | 6800 | 6500 | 5600 | 4800 | 4000 | 3200 | 2300 | 1400 |
| F | 7400 | 7100 | 6800 | 6500 | 6100 | 5300 | 4700 | 3900 | 3000 | 2300 | 1300 |
| G | 6900 | 6700 | 6400 | 6100 | 5800 | 5100 | 4600 | 3800 | 2900 | 2200 | 1300 |
| H | 6500 | 6200 | 5900 | 5600 | 5300 | 4900 | 4400 | 3600 | 2800 | 2100 | 1200 |
| I | 5600 | 5400 | 5200 | 5000 | 4700 | 4400 | 3900 | 3400 | 2700 | 2000 | 1200 |
| J | 4700 | 4500 | 4300 | 4100 | 3900 | 3700 | 3400 | 2900 | 2500 | 1800 | 1100 |
| K | 3900 | 3800 | 3700 | 3600 | 3400 | 3200 | 2900 | 2500 | 2200 | 1500 | 1100 |
| L | 3300 | 3200 | 3100 | 3000 | 2800 | 2600 | 2400 | 2100 | 1800 | 1300 | 1000 |
| M | 2600 | 2500 | 2400 | 2400 | 2300 | 2100 | 1900 | 1800 | 1400 | 1200 | 800 |

Please use these figures only as a point of comparison.
These prices are the author's opinion. B.J. Tadena
assumes no liability and makes no guarantees as to the
accuracy of these charts. For updated and accurate industry
price, refer to the Rapaport Diamond Report.

# *Price Guide*

SHAPE: ROUND        CARAT: 1 ½ or 1.5

| | IF | VVS1 | VVS2 | VS1 | VS2 | S11 | S12 | S13 | I1 | I2 | I3 |
|---|---|---|---|---|---|---|---|---|---|---|---|
| | | | | 1.50 to 1.99 ct | | | | | | | |
| D | 18000 | 12200 | 11100 | 9400 | 8400 | 7500 | 6400 | 5200 | 3900 | 2800 | 1600 |
| E | 12200 | 11200 | 9600 | 9000 | 8200 | 7300 | 6200 | 5000 | 3800 | 2700 | 1500 |
| F | 11200 | 9600 | 9000 | 8500 | 7900 | 7000 | 5900 | 4800 | 3700 | 2600 | 1500 |
| G | 9500 | 8800 | 8300 | 7900 | 7400 | 6700 | 5600 | 4600 | 3600 | 2500 | 1400 |
| H | 0100 | 7700 | 7400 | 7100 | 6800 | 6200 | 5200 | 4400 | 3500 | 2400 | 1400 |
| I | 7000 | 6800 | 6600 | 6400 | 6100 | 5500 | 4800 | 4200 | 3400 | 2300 | 1300 |
| J | 6200 | 6000 | 5800 | 5600 | 5200 | 4800 | 4300 | 3800 | 3200 | 2200 | 1300 |
| K | 5500 | 5300 | 5100 | 4900 | 4600 | 4300 | 3900 | 3500 | 2900 | 2000 | 1200 |
| L | 4700 | 4500 | 4300 | 4100 | 3900 | 3700 | 3400 | 3100 | 2600 | 1900 | 1100 |
| M | 4000 | 3900 | 3800 | 3600 | 3300 | 3000 | 2800 | 2600 | 2200 | 1700 | 1100 |

EMERALD        CARAT: 1 ½ or 1.5

| | IF | VVS1 | VVS2 | VS1 | VS2 | S11 | S12 | S13 | I1 | I2 | I3 |
|---|---|---|---|---|---|---|---|---|---|---|---|
| | | | | 1.50 to 1.99 ct | | | | | | | |
| D | 12800 | 8300 | 7400 | 7100 | 6700 | 5900 | 4900 | 4000 | 3200 | 2300 | 1300 |
| E | 8200 | 7400 | 7000 | 6700 | 6500 | 5700 | 4800 | 3900 | 3100 | 2200 | 1300 |
| F | 7300 | 7100 | 6800 | 6500 | 6100 | 5500 | 4700 | 3800 | 3000 | 2100 | 1200 |
| G | 6800 | 6600 | 6300 | 6000 | 5600 | 5100 | 4500 | 3700 | 2900 | 2000 | 1200 |
| H | 5900 | 5800 | 5600 | 5300 | 5000 | 4500 | 4000 | 3500 | 2800 | 1900 | 1100 |
| I | 5100 | 5000 | 4800 | 4500 | 4300 | 4000 | 3600 | 3200 | 2600 | 1800 | 1100 |
| J | 4600 | 4500 | 4300 | 4100 | 3900 | 3500 | 3200 | 2700 | 2300 | 1600 | 1000 |
| K | 3900 | 3800 | 3700 | 3500 | 3300 | 3100 | 2900 | 2500 | 2200 | 1500 | 1000 |
| L | 3200 | 3100 | 3000 | 2900 | 2800 | 2600 | 2300 | 2000 | 1800 | 1300 | 1000 |
| M | 2700 | 2600 | 2500 | 2400 | 2300 | 2100 | 1900 | 1800 | 1500 | 1300 | 800 |

Please use these figures only as a point of comparison.
These prices are the author's opinion. B.J. Tadena
assumes no liability and makes no guarantees as to the
accuracy of these charts. For updated and accurate industry
price, refer to the Rapaport Diamond Report.

# *Price Guide*

PEAR                       CARAT: 1 ½ or 1.5

| 1.50 to 1.99 ct | | | | | | | | | | |
|---|---|---|---|---|---|---|---|---|---|---|
| | IF | VVS1 | VVS2 | VS1 | VS2 | S11 | S12 | S13 | I1 | I2 | I3 |
| D | 14200 | 9200 | 8200 | 7700 | 7300 | 6500 | 5500 | 4500 | 3500 | 2500 | 1400 |
| E | 9200 | 8200 | 7700 | 7300 | 7000 | 6300 | 5400 | 4400 | 3400 | 2400 | 1400 |
| F | 8200 | 7700 | 7300 | 7000 | 6700 | 6000 | 5200 | 4300 | 3300 | 2300 | 1300 |
| G | 7700 | 7300 | 6900 | 6600 | 6300 | 5700 | 5000 | 4200 | 3200 | 2200 | 1300 |
| H | 6800 | 6500 | 6200 | 5900 | 5600 | 5100 | 4500 | 4000 | 3100 | 2100 | 1200 |
| I | 5800 | 5600 | 5400 | 5100 | 4900 | 4500 | 4100 | 3700 | 2900 | 2000 | 1200 |
| J | 5000 | 4900 | 4700 | 4500 | 4300 | 4000 | 3600 | 3100 | 2600 | 1800 | 1100 |
| K | 4200 | 4100 | 4000 | 3800 | 3600 | 3400 | 3100 | 2700 | 2300 | 1600 | 1100 |
| L | 3500 | 3400 | 3300 | 3200 | 3000 | 2800 | 2500 | 2200 | 1900 | 1400 | 1000 |
| M | 2800 | 2700 | 2600 | 2500 | 2400 | 2200 | 2000 | 1900 | 1500 | 1300 | 800 |

MARQUISE               CARAT: 1 ½ or 1.5

| 1.50 to 1.99 ct | | | | | | | | | | |
|---|---|---|---|---|---|---|---|---|---|---|
| | IF | VVS1 | VVS2 | VS1 | VS2 | S11 | S12 | S13 | I1 | I2 | I3 |
| D | 14200 | 9200 | 8200 | 7800 | 7500 | 6600 | 5600 | 4700 | 3700 | 2600 | 1500 |
| E | 9200 | 8200 | 7800 | 7500 | 7300 | 6500 | 5600 | 4600 | 3600 | 2500 | 1500 |
| F | 8200 | 7800 | 7400 | 7300 | 7000 | 6300 | 5400 | 4500 | 3500 | 2400 | 1400 |
| G | 7800 | 7400 | 7100 | 6900 | 6600 | 6000 | 5200 | 4400 | 3400 | 2300 | 1400 |
| H | 7000 | 6800 | 6500 | 6200 | 5900 | 5400 | 4800 | 4300 | 3300 | 2200 | 1300 |
| I | 6000 | 5800 | 5600 | 5400 | 5200 | 4800 | 4400 | 4000 | 3100 | 2100 | 1300 |
| J | 5200 | 5100 | 4900 | 4700 | 4500 | 4200 | 3800 | 3300 | 2700 | 1900 | 1200 |
| K | 4400 | 4300 | 4200 | 4000 | 3800 | 3600 | 3300 | 2900 | 2500 | 1800 | 1200 |
| L | 3600 | 3500 | 3400 | 3300 | 3100 | 2900 | 2600 | 2300 | 2000 | 1500 | 1100 |
| M | 2900 | 2800 | 2700 | 2600 | 2500 | 2300 | 2100 | 2000 | 1600 | 1400 | 900 |

Please use these figures only as a point of comparison.
These prices are the author's opinion. B.J. Tadena
assumes no liability and makes no guarantees as to the
accuracy of these charts. For updated and accurate industry
price, refer to the Rapaport Diamond Report.

# *Price Guide*

SHAPE: ROUND        CARAT: 2.00

| | | | | | 2.00 to 2.99 ct | | | | | | |
|---|---|---|---|---|---|---|---|---|---|---|---|
| | IF | VVS1 | VVS2 | VS1 | VS2 | S11 | S12 | S13 | I1 | I2 | I3 |
| D | 26200 | 19200 | 16800 | 13500 | 10800 | 8900 | 7200 | 5700 | 4300 | 3100 | 1800 |
| E | 19200 | 16800 | 13500 | 11800 | 10400 | 8700 | 7000 | 5500 | 4200 | 3000 | 1700 |
| F | 16800 | 13500 | 11800 | 10600 | 10000 | 8400 | 6800 | 5400 | 4100 | 2900 | 1600 |
| G | 13300 | 11800 | 10500 | 10000 | 9400 | 8000 | 6600 | 5300 | 4000 | 2800 | 1600 |
| H | 11300 | 9900 | 9300 | 8800 | 8200 | 7200 | 6100 | 5000 | 3900 | 2700 | 1500 |
| I | 8800 | 8500 | 8100 | 7600 | 7100 | 6300 | 5500 | 4700 | 3800 | 2600 | 1400 |
| J | 7500 | 7200 | 6900 | 6400 | 6000 | 5400 | 4900 | 4400 | 3700 | 2400 | 1400 |
| K | 6200 | 6000 | 5800 | 5600 | 5300 | 4900 | 4500 | 4100 | 3400 | 2300 | 1300 |
| L | 5300 | 5100 | 4900 | 4700 | 4400 | 4100 | 3800 | 3400 | 3000 | 2200 | 1200 |
| M | 4500 | 4300 | 4100 | 3800 | 3600 | 3300 | 3100 | 2900 | 2500 | 2000 | 1200 |

EMERALD        CARAT: 2.00

| | | | | | 2.00 to 2.99 ct | | | | | | |
|---|---|---|---|---|---|---|---|---|---|---|---|
| | IF | VVS1 | VVS2 | VS1 | VS2 | S11 | S12 | S13 | I1 | I2 | I3 |
| D | 20100 | 12800 | 11500 | 10500 | 9600 | 7400 | 5600 | 4500 | 3700 | 2300 | 1400 |
| E | 12600 | 11500 | 10300 | 9800 | 8600 | 7100 | 5400 | 4300 | 3500 | 2300 | 1400 |
| F | 11300 | 10300 | 9600 | 8600 | 7900 | 6700 | 5300 | 4200 | 3300 | 2200 | 1400 |
| G | 10000 | 9600 | 8400 | 7900 | 7300 | 6200 | 5000 | 3900 | 3200 | 2100 | 1300 |
| H | 9200 | 8200 | 7300 | 6900 | 6100 | 5300 | 4500 | 3700 | 3000 | 2000 | 1200 |
| I | 7100 | 6800 | 6300 | 5700 | 5000 | 4600 | 4000 | 3400 | 2700 | 1900 | 1200 |
| J | 5700 | 5400 | 5100 | 4800 | 4300 | 4000 | 3400 | 3000 | 2500 | 1800 | 1100 |
| K | 4600 | 4300 | 4100 | 4000 | 3700 | 3400 | 3100 | 2600 | 2300 | 1700 | 1100 |
| L | 3700 | 3500 | 3300 | 3200 | 2900 | 2700 | 2500 | 2200 | 1900 | 1500 | 1000 |
| M | 3000 | 2900 | 2700 | 2600 | 2400 | 2300 | 2100 | 1900 | 1600 | 1400 | 800 |

Please use these figures only as a point of comparison.
These prices are the author's opinion. B.J. Tadena
assumes no liability and makes no guarantees as to the
accuracy of these charts. For updated and accurate industry
price, refer to the Rapaport Diamond Report.

# *Price Guide*

PEAR                      CARAT: 2.00

| | | | | | 2.00 to 2.99 ct | | | | | | |
|---|---|---|---|---|---|---|---|---|---|---|---|
| | IF | VVS1 | VVS2 | VS1 | VS2 | S11 | S12 | S13 | I1 | I2 | I3 |
| D | 21200 | 14300 | 12900 | 11500 | 10500 | 8200 | 6200 | 5200 | 4100 | 2700 | 1600 |
| E | 14300 | 12900 | 11500 | 10700 | 9400 | 7900 | 6000 | 4900 | 3900 | 2600 | 1500 |
| F | 12900 | 11500 | 10700 | 9400 | 8800 | 7500 | 5800 | 4700 | 3700 | 2400 | 1500 |
| G | 11500 | 10700 | 9400 | 8800 | 8100 | 6900 | 5500 | 4500 | 3500 | 2300 | 1400 |
| H | 10700 | 9300 | 8200 | 7700 | 6900 | 6100 | 5000 | 4200 | 3300 | 2200 | 1300 |
| I | 8200 | 7700 | 7200 | 6500 | 5900 | 5300 | 4600 | 3900 | 3000 | 2100 | 1300 |
| J | 6400 | 6100 | 5800 | 5400 | 4900 | 4500 | 3900 | 3400 | 2800 | 2000 | 1200 |
| K | 5200 | 4900 | 4700 | 4500 | 4200 | 3900 | 3500 | 3000 | 2500 | 1900 | 1200 |
| L | 4200 | 4000 | 3800 | 3600 | 3300 | 3100 | 2900 | 2500 | 2100 | 1700 | 1100 |
| M | 3400 | 3300 | 3100 | 3000 | 2800 | 2600 | 2400 | 2200 | 1800 | 1500 | 900 |

MARQUISE                  CARAT: 2.00

| | | | | | 2.00 to 2.99 ct | | | | | | |
|---|---|---|---|---|---|---|---|---|---|---|---|
| | IF | VVS1 | VVS2 | VS1 | VS2 | S11 | S12 | S13 | I1 | I2 | I3 |
| D | 21200 | 14300 | 12900 | 11500 | 10700 | 8500 | 6500 | 5400 | 4100 | 2700 | 1600 |
| E | 14300 | 12900 | 11500 | 10700 | 9700 | 8200 | 6300 | 5100 | 4000 | 2600 | 1600 |
| F | 12900 | 11500 | 10700 | 9700 | 9100 | 7800 | 6100 | 4900 | 3900 | 2500 | 1500 |
| G | 11500 | 10700 | 9700 | 9100 | 8400 | 7200 | 5800 | 4700 | 3700 | 2400 | 1500 |
| H | 10700 | 9600 | 8500 | 8000 | 7200 | 6400 | 5300 | 4400 | 3500 | 2300 | 1400 |
| I | 8400 | 7900 | 7400 | 6700 | 6200 | 5600 | 4800 | 4100 | 3200 | 2200 | 1400 |
| J | 6600 | 6300 | 6000 | 5600 | 5200 | 4800 | 4100 | 3600 | 3000 | 2000 | 1300 |
| K | 5400 | 5100 | 4900 | 4700 | 4400 | 4100 | 3600 | 3100 | 2600 | 1900 | 1300 |
| L | 4400 | 4200 | 4000 | 3800 | 3400 | 3200 | 3000 | 2500 | 2100 | 1700 | 1200 |
| M | 3500 | 3400 | 3200 | 3100 | 2900 | 2700 | 2400 | 2200 | 1800 | 1500 | 1000 |

Please use these figures only as a point of comparison.
These prices are the author's opinion. B.J. Tadena
assumes no liability and makes no guarantees as to the
accuracy of these charts. For updated and accurate industry
price, refer to the Rapaport Diamond Report.

# *Price Guide*

SHAPE: ROUND          CARAT: 3.00

| | IF | VVS1 | VVS2 | VS1 | VS2 | S11 | S12 | S13 | I1 | I2 | I3 |
|---|---|---|---|---|---|---|---|---|---|---|---|
| | | | | 3.00 to 3.99 ct | | | | | | | |
| D | 40500 | 28600 | 24300 | 18800 | 15300 | 12500 | 9200 | 7900 | 6800 | 3700 | 2000 |
| E | 28600 | 24300 | 18800 | 15300 | 13600 | 11700 | 8700 | 7500 | 6300 | 3600 | 1900 |
| F | 24300 | 18800 | 15300 | 13600 | 12700 | 10900 | 8300 | 7100 | 5900 | 3400 | 1800 |
| G | 18700 | 15300 | 13600 | 12700 | 11100 | 9700 | 7800 | 6700 | 5600 | 3200 | 1700 |
| H | 15000 | 13200 | 12200 | 11000 | 9600 | 8200 | 7300 | 6200 | 5200 | 3000 | 1700 |
| I | 11700 | 10700 | 10200 | 9400 | 8000 | 7300 | 6400 | 5600 | 4800 | 2900 | 1600 |
| J | 9700 | 9200 | 8800 | 8000 | 7200 | 6600 | 5900 | 5200 | 4400 | 2700 | 1500 |
| K | 8600 | 8200 | 7700 | 7000 | 6400 | 5800 | 5100 | 4600 | 4100 | 2500 | 1500 |
| L | 7000 | 6700 | 6300 | 5800 | 5300 | 4700 | 4100 | 3700 | 3200 | 2400 | 1400 |
| M | 5700 | 5500 | 5300 | 4900 | 4600 | 4100 | 3600 | 3300 | 2800 | 2200 | 1400 |

EMERALD          CARAT: 3.00

| | IF | VVS1 | VVS2 | VS1 | VS2 | S11 | S12 | S13 | I1 | I2 | I3 |
|---|---|---|---|---|---|---|---|---|---|---|---|
| | | | | 3.00 to 3.99 ct | | | | | | | |
| D | 28100 | 19100 | 16700 | 15200 | 13300 | 11300 | 7900 | 7000 | 6000 | 3200 | 1800 |
| E | 19100 | 16700 | 14900 | 13300 | 12200 | 10600 | 7500 | 6500 | 5600 | 3000 | 1700 |
| F | 16300 | 14900 | 13100 | 12200 | 11300 | 9800 | 7100 | 6100 | 5200 | 2800 | 1600 |
| G | 14500 | 13100 | 11900 | 11300 | 9900 | 8600 | 6800 | 5800 | 5000 | 2600 | 1500 |
| H | 12500 | 11700 | 10400 | 9800 | 8500 | 7100 | 6400 | 5400 | 4500 | 2400 | 1400 |
| I | 10200 | 9500 | 9000 | 8300 | 6900 | 6300 | 5400 | 4700 | 4100 | 2300 | 1400 |
| J | 7700 | 7300 | 6800 | 6400 | 5900 | 5200 | 4500 | 3900 | 3300 | 2100 | 1300 |
| K | 6200 | 5900 | 5600 | 5100 | 4900 | 4400 | 3800 | 3400 | 3000 | 1900 | 1200 |
| L | 4900 | 4700 | 4400 | 4100 | 4000 | 3500 | 3200 | 2800 | 2400 | 1700 | 1100 |
| M | 3500 | 3300 | 3200 | 3100 | 2900 | 2600 | 2300 | 2200 | 2000 | 1600 | 900 |

Please use these figures only as a point of comparison.
These prices are the author's opinion. B.J. Tadena
assumes no liability and makes no guarantees as to the
accuracy of these charts. For updated and accurate industry
price, refer to the Rapaport Diamond Report.

# Price Guide

PEAR                    CARAT: 3.00

| | | | | | 3.00 to 3.99 ct | | | | | |
|---|---|---|---|---|---|---|---|---|---|---|---|
| | IF | VVS1 | VVS2 | VS1 | VS2 | S11 | S12 | S13 | I1 | I2 | I3 |
| D | 29700 | 21400 | 18400 | 16400 | 14400 | 12200 | 8500 | 7800 | 6700 | 3500 | 2000 |
| E | 21400 | 18400 | 16400 | 14400 | 13100 | 11400 | 8000 | 7300 | 6200 | 3300 | 1900 |
| F | 18400 | 16400 | 14400 | 13100 | 12200 | 10500 | 7600 | 6800 | 5800 | 3100 | 1800 |
| G | 16400 | 14400 | 13100 | 12200 | 10600 | 9200 | 7300 | 6400 | 5500 | 2900 | 1700 |
| H | 14200 | 13000 | 11500 | 10600 | 9200 | 7700 | 7000 | 6000 | 5000 | 2700 | 1600 |
| I | 11500 | 10500 | 10000 | 9200 | 7700 | 7000 | 6000 | 5300 | 4500 | 2500 | 1500 |
| J | 8600 | 8100 | 7600 | 7100 | 6600 | 5800 | 5000 | 4400 | 3700 | 2300 | 1400 |
| K | 6900 | 6600 | 6200 | 5700 | 5400 | 4900 | 4200 | 3800 | 3300 | 2100 | 1300 |
| L | 5400 | 5200 | 4900 | 4600 | 4400 | 3900 | 3500 | 3100 | 2700 | 1900 | 1200 |
| M | 3900 | 3700 | 3600 | 3400 | 3200 | 2900 | 2600 | 2400 | 2200 | 1800 | 1000 |

MARQUISE                CARAT: 3.00

| | | | | | 3.00 to 3.99 ct | | | | | |
|---|---|---|---|---|---|---|---|---|---|---|---|
| | IF | VVS1 | VVS2 | VS1 | VS2 | S11 | S12 | S13 | I1 | I2 | I3 |
| D | 29700 | 21400 | 18400 | 16400 | 14400 | 12200 | 8500 | 7800 | 6700 | 3500 | 2000 |
| E | 21400 | 18400 | 16400 | 14400 | 13100 | 11400 | 8000 | 7300 | 6200 | 3300 | 1900 |
| F | 18400 | 16400 | 14400 | 13100 | 12200 | 10500 | 7600 | 6800 | 5800 | 3100 | 1800 |
| G | 16400 | 14400 | 13100 | 12200 | 10600 | 9200 | 7300 | 6400 | 5500 | 2900 | 1700 |
| H | 14200 | 13000 | 11500 | 10600 | 9200 | 7700 | 7000 | 6000 | 5000 | 2700 | 1600 |
| I | 11500 | 10500 | 10000 | 9200 | 7700 | 7000 | 6000 | 5300 | 4500 | 2500 | 1500 |
| J | 8600 | 8100 | 7600 | 7100 | 6600 | 5800 | 5000 | 4400 | 3700 | 2300 | 1400 |
| K | 6900 | 6600 | 6200 | 5700 | 5400 | 4900 | 4200 | 3800 | 3300 | 2200 | 1400 |
| L | 5400 | 5200 | 4900 | 4600 | 4400 | 3900 | 3500 | 3100 | 2700 | 1900 | 1300 |
| M | 3900 | 3700 | 3600 | 3400 | 3200 | 2900 | 2600 | 2400 | 2200 | 1800 | 1100 |

Please use these figures only as a point of comparison.
These prices are the author's opinion. B.J. Tadena
assumes no liability and makes no guarantees as to the
accuracy of these charts. For updated and accurate industry
price, refer to the Rapaport Diamond Report.

# *Price Guide*

SHAPE: ROUND          CARAT: 4.00

| | | | | | 4.00 to 4.99 ct | | | | | | |
|---|---|---|---|---|---|---|---|---|---|---|---|
| | IF | VVS1 | VVS2 | VS1 | VS2 | S11 | S12 | S13 | I1 | I2 | I3 |
| D | 42500 | 30900 | 26300 | 20400 | 16900 | 13800 | 9900 | 8600 | 7400 | 4200 | 2100 |
| E | 30900 | 26400 | 20400 | 16900 | 15000 | 12800 | 9300 | 8100 | 6900 | 4100 | 2000 |
| F | 26400 | 20400 | 16900 | 14900 | 13900 | 11800 | 8900 | 7600 | 6500 | 3900 | 1900 |
| G | 20400 | 16900 | 14900 | 13900 | 12000 | 10300 | 8500 | 7200 | 6100 | 3700 | 1800 |
| H | 16100 | 14600 | 13100 | 11800 | 10200 | 9100 | 7800 | 6700 | 5700 | 3500 | 1800 |
| I | 12600 | 11600 | 10800 | 10200 | 9400 | 8100 | 7200 | 6300 | 5400 | 3300 | 1700 |
| J | 10000 | 9500 | 9000 | 8500 | 8000 | 7100 | 6500 | 5700 | 4900 | 3100 | 1600 |
| K | 8800 | 8400 | 8000 | 7400 | 6800 | 6100 | 5600 | 5000 | 4400 | 2800 | 1500 |
| L | 7100 | 6800 | 6500 | 6200 | 5700 | 5100 | 4500 | 4100 | 3600 | 2600 | 1400 |
| M | 5900 | 5700 | 5500 | 5300 | 5000 | 4500 | 4000 | 3600 | 3200 | 2400 | 1400 |

EMERALD          CARAT: 4.00

| | | | | | 4.00 to 4.99 ct | | | | | | |
|---|---|---|---|---|---|---|---|---|---|---|---|
| | IF | VVS1 | VVS2 | VS1 | VS2 | S11 | S12 | S13 | I1 | I2 | I3 |
| D | 30100 | 20600 | 18000 | 16600 | 14700 | 12200 | 8800 | 7700 | 6600 | 3600 | 1900 |
| E | 20600 | 18000 | 16200 | 14700 | 13200 | 11600 | 8400 | 7200 | 6100 | 3300 | 1800 |
| F | 17600 | 16200 | 14400 | 13200 | 12000 | 10700 | 8000 | 6800 | 5800 | 3200 | 1700 |
| G | 15900 | 14400 | 12700 | 12000 | 10700 | 9300 | 7600 | 6400 | 5400 | 3000 | 1600 |
| H | 13600 | 12600 | 11300 | 10600 | 9200 | 8300 | 6900 | 5900 | 5000 | 2800 | 1500 |
| I | 10700 | 9900 | 9500 | 9000 | 8100 | 7200 | 5900 | 5100 | 4300 | 2600 | 1400 |
| J | 8200 | 7700 | 7300 | 6800 | 6400 | 5900 | 5000 | 4400 | 3800 | 2400 | 1400 |
| K | 6700 | 6300 | 5900 | 5700 | 5300 | 5000 | 4500 | 4000 | 3400 | 2200 | 1300 |
| L | 5300 | 5100 | 5000 | 4700 | 4500 | 4100 | 3400 | 3100 | 2800 | 2000 | 1200 |
| M | 4100 | 4000 | 3800 | 3600 | 3400 | 3200 | 2700 | 2400 | 2300 | 1800 | 1000 |

Please use these figures only as a point of comparison.
These prices are the author's opinion. B.J. Tadena
assumes no liability and makes no guarantees as to the
accuracy of these charts. For updated and accurate industry
price, refer to the Rapaport Diamond Report.

137

# *Price Guide*

PEAR                    CARAT: 4.0

| | | | | | | | | | | | |
|---|---|---|---|---|---|---|---|---|---|---|---|
| | \multicolumn{11}{c}{4.00 to 4.99 ct} | | | | | | | | | | |

| | IF | VVS1 | VVS2 | VS1 | VS2 | S11 | S12 | S13 | I1 | I2 | I3 |
|---|---|---|---|---|---|---|---|---|---|---|---|
| D | 31500 | 22900 | 19900 | 17900 | 15900 | 13200 | 9500 | 8500 | 7300 | 4000 | 2100 |
| E | 22900 | 19900 | 17900 | 15900 | 14200 | 12500 | 9000 | 8000 | 6800 | 3700 | 2000 |
| F | 19900 | 17900 | 15900 | 14200 | 12900 | 11500 | 8600 | 7600 | 6400 | 3500 | 1900 |
| G | 17900 | 15900 | 14000 | 12900 | 11500 | 10000 | 8200 | 7100 | 6000 | 3300 | 1800 |
| H | 15400 | 14000 | 12500 | 11500 | 10000 | 9000 | 7500 | 6600 | 5600 | 3100 | 1700 |
| I | 12000 | 11000 | 10500 | 10000 | 9000 | 8000 | 6500 | 5700 | 4800 | 2900 | 1600 |
| J | 9100 | 8600 | 8100 | 7600 | 7100 | 6500 | 5500 | 4900 | 4200 | 2700 | 1500 |
| K | 7400 | 7000 | 6600 | 6300 | 5900 | 5500 | 5000 | 4400 | 3800 | 2400 | 1400 |
| L | 5900 | 5700 | 5500 | 5200 | 5000 | 4500 | 3800 | 3500 | 3100 | 2200 | 1300 |
| M | 4600 | 4400 | 4200 | 4000 | 3800 | 3500 | 3000 | 2700 | 2500 | 2000 | 1100 |

MARQUISE                CARAT: 4.00

| | \multicolumn{11}{c}{4.00 to 4.99 ct} | | | | | | | | | | |
|---|---|---|---|---|---|---|---|---|---|---|---|

| | IF | VVS1 | VVS2 | VS1 | VS2 | S11 | S12 | S13 | I1 | I2 | I3 |
|---|---|---|---|---|---|---|---|---|---|---|---|
| D | 31500 | 22900 | 19900 | 17900 | 15900 | 13200 | 9500 | 8500 | 7300 | 4000 | 2100 |
| E | 22900 | 19900 | 17900 | 15900 | 14200 | 12500 | 9000 | 8000 | 6800 | 3700 | 2000 |
| F | 19900 | 17900 | 15900 | 14200 | 12900 | 11500 | 8600 | 7600 | 6400 | 3500 | 1900 |
| G | 17900 | 15900 | 14000 | 12900 | 11500 | 10000 | 8200 | 7100 | 6000 | 3300 | 1800 |
| H | 15400 | 14000 | 12500 | 11500 | 10000 | 9000 | 7500 | 6600 | 5600 | 3100 | 1700 |
| I | 12000 | 11000 | 10500 | 10000 | 9000 | 8000 | 6500 | 5700 | 4800 | 2900 | 1600 |
| J | 9100 | 8600 | 8100 | 7600 | 7100 | 6500 | 5500 | 4900 | 4200 | 2700 | 1500 |
| K | 7400 | 7000 | 6600 | 6300 | 5900 | 5500 | 5000 | 4400 | 3800 | 2400 | 1500 |
| L | 5900 | 5700 | 5500 | 5200 | 5000 | 4500 | 3800 | 3500 | 3100 | 2200 | 1400 |
| M | 4600 | 4400 | 4200 | 4000 | 3800 | 3500 | 3000 | 2700 | 2500 | 2000 | 1200 |

Please use these figures only as a point of comparison.
These prices are the author's opinion. B.J. Tadena
assumes no liability and makes no guarantees as to the
accuracy of these charts. For updated and accurate industry
price, refer to the Rapaport Diamond Report.

# Price Guide

SHAPE: ROUND          CARAT: 5.00

| | | | | | 5.00 to 5.99 ct | | | | | | |
|---|---|---|---|---|---|---|---|---|---|---|---|
| | IF | VVS1 | VVS2 | VS1 | VS2 | S11 | S12 | S13 | I1 | I2 | I3 |
| D | 56500 | 39500 | 34000 | 28000 | 23000 | 19300 | 13300 | 10700 | 8100 | 4700 | 2400 |
| E | 39500 | 34000 | 28000 | 24000 | 21000 | 17300 | 12800 | 10100 | 7600 | 4500 | 2200 |
| F | 34000 | 28000 | 24500 | 21500 | 18500 | 15300 | 12300 | 9700 | 7300 | 4300 | 2100 |
| G | 27900 | 24500 | 21500 | 18500 | 16200 | 14000 | 11500 | 9200 | 6900 | 4100 | 2000 |
| H | 23200 | 20600 | 18200 | 15900 | 14000 | 11900 | 9800 | 8200 | 6400 | 3900 | 1900 |
| I | 18100 | 17100 | 15900 | 13800 | 12200 | 9800 | 8600 | 7200 | 5800 | 3700 | 1800 |
| J | 12700 | 12200 | 11700 | 11200 | 9800 | 8200 | 7300 | 6300 | 5300 | 3500 | 1700 |
| K | 10100 | 9700 | 9200 | 8700 | 8100 | 7200 | 6100 | 5500 | 4800 | 3200 | 1700 |
| L | 8300 | 7800 | 7400 | 6900 | 6400 | 5900 | 5100 | 4700 | 4200 | 2900 | 1600 |
| M | 6800 | 6500 | 6200 | 5900 | 5500 | 5100 | 4600 | 4100 | 3600 | 2600 | 1600 |

EMERALD          CARAT: 5.00

| | | | | | 5.00 to 5.99 ct | | | | | | |
|---|---|---|---|---|---|---|---|---|---|---|---|
| | IF | VVS1 | VVS2 | VS1 | VS2 | S11 | S12 | S13 | I1 | I2 | I3 |
| D | 44600 | 27600 | 25100 | 23100 | 20800 | 17100 | 11600 | 9400 | 7200 | 4000 | 2200 |
| E | 27600 | 25100 | 22600 | 20800 | 18800 | 15700 | 11100 | 9000 | 6800 | 3800 | 2000 |
| F | 25100 | 22600 | 20400 | 18800 | 16300 | 13900 | 10700 | 8600 | 6500 | 3600 | 1800 |
| G | 22100 | 20400 | 18100 | 16300 | 14400 | 12500 | 10200 | 8100 | 6100 | 3400 | 1700 |
| H | 19000 | 17600 | 15300 | 14300 | 12400 | 10600 | 8700 | 7200 | 5600 | 3200 | 1600 |
| I | 14000 | 13200 | 12800 | 11700 | 10400 | 8600 | 7200 | 6300 | 5100 | 3100 | 1500 |
| J | 10400 | 9900 | 9500 | 9000 | 8100 | 7200 | 6300 | 5600 | 4700 | 2800 | 1400 |
| K | 8300 | 7900 | 7700 | 7200 | 6800 | 6300 | 5400 | 4900 | 4200 | 2500 | 1400 |
| L | 6400 | 6200 | 6100 | 5900 | 5600 | 5100 | 4300 | 4100 | 3800 | 2300 | 1300 |
| M | 4800 | 4600 | 4400 | 4200 | 3900 | 3700 | 3400 | 3100 | 2700 | 2000 | 1200 |

Please use these figures only as a point of comparison.
These prices arc the author's opinion. B.J. Tadena
assumes no liability and makes no guarantees as to the
accuracy of these charts. For updated and accurate industry
price, refer to the Rapaport Diamond Report.

# *Price Guide*

PEAR                     CARAT: 5.00

| 5.00 to 5.99 ct | | | | | | | | | | |
|---|---|---|---|---|---|---|---|---|---|---|
| | IF | VVS1 | VVS2 | VS1 | VS2 | S11 | S12 | S13 | I1 | I2 | I3 |
| D | 44500 | 31000 | 28000 | 25000 | 22500 | 18500 | 12500 | 10500 | 8000 | 4400 | 2400 |
| E | 30900 | 28000 | 25000 | 22500 | 20300 | 17000 | 12000 | 10000 | 7500 | 4200 | 2200 |
| F | 27900 | 25000 | 22500 | 20300 | 17600 | 15000 | 11500 | 9500 | 7200 | 4000 | 2000 |
| G | 24900 | 22500 | 20000 | 17600 | 15500 | 13500 | 11000 | 9000 | 6800 | 3800 | 1900 |
| H | 21500 | 19500 | 17000 | 15500 | 13500 | 11500 | 9500 | 8000 | 6200 | 3600 | 1800 |
| I | 15700 | 14700 | 14200 | 13000 | 11500 | 9500 | 8000 | 7000 | 5700 | 3400 | 1700 |
| J | 11500 | 11000 | 10500 | 10000 | 9000 | 8000 | 7000 | 6200 | 5200 | 3100 | 1600 |
| K | 9200 | 8800 | 8500 | 8000 | 7500 | 7000 | 6000 | 5400 | 4700 | 2800 | 1500 |
| L | 7100 | 6900 | 6800 | 6600 | 6200 | 5700 | 4800 | 4600 | 4200 | 2500 | 1400 |
| M | 5300 | 5100 | 4900 | 4700 | 4500 | 4200 | 3800 | 3400 | 3000 | 2200 | 1300 |

MARQUISE             CARAT: 5.00

| 5.00 to 54.99 ct | | | | | | | | | | |
|---|---|---|---|---|---|---|---|---|---|---|
| | IF | VVS1 | VVS2 | VS1 | VS2 | S11 | S12 | S13 | I1 | I2 | I3 |
| D | 44500 | 31000 | 28000 | 25000 | 22500 | 18500 | 12500 | 10500 | 8000 | 4400 | 2400 |
| E | 30900 | 28000 | 25000 | 22500 | 20300 | 17000 | 12000 | 10000 | 7500 | 4200 | 2200 |
| F | 27900 | 25000 | 22500 | 20300 | 17600 | 15000 | 11500 | 9500 | 7200 | 4000 | 2000 |
| G | 24900 | 22500 | 20000 | 17600 | 15500 | 13500 | 11000 | 9000 | 6800 | 3800 | 1900 |
| H | 21500 | 19500 | 17000 | 15500 | 13500 | 11500 | 9500 | 8000 | 6200 | 3600 | 1800 |
| I | 15700 | 14700 | 14200 | 13000 | 11500 | 9500 | 8000 | 7000 | 5700 | 3400 | 1700 |
| J | 11500 | 11000 | 10500 | 10000 | 9000 | 8000 | 7000 | 6200 | 5200 | 3100 | 1600 |
| K | 9200 | 8800 | 8500 | 8000 | 7500 | 7000 | 6000 | 5400 | 4700 | 2800 | 1600 |
| L | 7100 | 6900 | 6800 | 6600 | 6200 | 5700 | 4800 | 4600 | 4200 | 2500 | 1500 |
| M | 5300 | 5100 | 4900 | 4700 | 4500 | 4200 | 3800 | 3400 | 3000 | 2200 | 1300 |

Please use these figures only as a point of comparison.
These prices are the author's opinion. B.J. Tadena
assumes no liability and makes no guarantees as to the
accuracy of these charts. For updated and accurate industry
price, refer to the Rapaport Diamond Report.

# APPENDIX C

## INTERNATIONALLY RECOGNIZED LABORATORIES
## FOR CERTIFICATION REPORTS
## OF AUTHENTICITY AND QUALITY

American Gemological Laboratory
580 Fifth Avenue, 12th Floor
New York, NY 10036
(Services available to the jewelry trade and to the public)

Colored Diamond Laboratory Services, Inc.
15 West 47th Street
New York, NY 10036
(Issuing reports on colored diamonds only)

Gemological Lab. Gubelin
Denkmalstrasse, 2
Ch-6006 Luzern, Switzerland
(Only to the jewelry trade)

GIA Gem Trade Laboratory
Gemological Institure of America
580 Fifth Avenue
New York, NY 10036
(Only to the jewelry trade)

GIA Gem Trade Laboratory
Gemological Institute of America
1660 Stewart Street
Santa Monica, CA 90404
(Only to the jewelry trade)

Hoge Raad voor Diamant (HRD)
Hoveniersstraat, 22
B-2018 Antwerp, Belgium

Schweizerische Stiftung fur Edelstein - Forschung (SSEF)
Lowenstrasse, 17
Ch-8001 Zurich, Switzerland

# APPENDIX D

## DIRECTORY OF GEMOLOGICAL LABORATORIES
## IN THE UNITED STATES

ALABAMA

Jimmy Smith Jewelers
Southland Plaza Shopping Center
Decatur, AL 35602
Tel. (205) 353-2512                    Jimmy Ray Smith (CGA)

Mason Jewelers
        3011 South Parkway
        Hunstville, AL 35801
        Tel. (205) 883-2150            Ronnie Robinson (CGA)
                also at
        5901-73 University Drive
        Madison Square Mall
        Huntsville, AL 35806
        Tel. (205) 830-5930            Emily White Ware (CGA)

Mickleboro's of Montgomery
3003-C McGehee Road
Montgomery, AL 36111
Tel. (205) 281-6597                    Amy J. Michaels (CGA)

Ware Jewelers
        111 So. College Street
        Auburn, AL 36830
        Tel. (205) 821-7375            Stanley Arlington (CGA)
                and at
        Village Mall
        162 Opelika Road
        Auburn, AL 36830
        Tel. (205) 821-3122            Ronnie Ware (CGA)

142

ARIZONA

Ambassador Diamond Brokers
4668 E. Speedway Blvd.
Tucson, AZ 85712
Tel. (602) 327-8800                                    Stewart M. Kruper (CMA)

Caldwell Jewelry Corp.
7225 N. Oracle Road
Tucson, AZ 85704
Tel. (602) 742-3687                                    Brenda J. Caldwell (MGA)

Dennis D. Naughton Jewelers
129 Park Central Mall
Phoenix, AZ 85013
Tel. (602) 264-2857                                    Net T. Burns (CGA)

Grunewald & Adams Jewelers
Biltmore Fashion Park
2468 E. Camelback
Phoenix, AZ 85016
Tel. (602) 955-8450                                    Sandra Overland (CGA)

Jim Anderson Jewelers
2112 N. Fourth Street
Flagstaff, AZ 86004
Tel. (602) 526-0074                                    James R. Anderson (CGA)

Joseph M. Berning Jewelers
130 E. University Drive
Tempe, AZ 85281
Tel. (602) 967-8917                                    Patricia Berning (CGA)

Marshall's Artistry in Gold, Inc.
4811 E. Grant Road, #113
Tucson, AZ 85712
Tel. (602) 325-9955                                    Richard G. Marshall (CGA)

Michelle Hallier (MGA)
1250 East Missouri St.
Phoenix, AZ 85014
Tel. (602) 277-9780

Molina Fine Jewelers
1250 E. Missouri St., #3
Phoenix, AZ 85014
Tel. (602) 265-5001                    Alfredo J. Molina (MGA)

Ouellet andLynch
5743 W. St. Johns Road
Glendale, AZ 85308
Tel. (602) 264-3210                    Craig A. Lynch (MGA)

Paul Johnson Jewelers
1940 E. Camelback Road
Phoenix, AZ 85016
Tel. (602) 277-1421                    Thomas Hergenroether (CGA)

Peterson's Jewelry
209 W. Gurley Street
Prescott, AZ 86301
Tel. (602) 445-3098                    James Lamerson (CGA)

Schmieder & Son Jewelers
Park Central Mall West
Phoenix, AZ 85013
Tel. (602) 264-4464                    Carl Schmieder (CGA)

Schmieder & Son Jewelers
10001 W. Bell Road
Sun City, AZ 85351
Tel. (602) 974-3627                    Robert Delane Cloutier (CGA)

Setterberg Jewelers
Campana Square
9885 West Bell Road
Sun City, AZ 85351
Tel. (602) 972-6130                    Wendell Setterberg (CGA)

## ARKANSAS

Stanley Jewelers
3422 John F. Kennedy Blvd.
North Little Rock, AK  72116
Tel. (501)  753-1081            Loyd C. Stanley (CGA)

Underwood's Jewelers
611 W. Dickson
Fayetteville, AK  72701
Tel. (501)  521-2000        William G. Underwood  (CGA)

## CALIFORNIA

A.L. Jacobs & Sons Jewelers
675 B. Street
San Diego, CA  92101
Tel. (619)  232-1418          Christopher Jacobs (CGA)

The Altobelli Jewelers
4419 Lankershim Blvd.
North Hollywood, CA  91602
Tel. (818)  763-5151            Cos Altobelli (CGA)

American Jewelry Co.
Oak Park Tower #500
3200 21$^{st}$ St. at Oak
Bakersfield, CA  93301
Tel. (805)  325-5023          Carl M. Saenger (CGA)

Azevedo Jewelers & Gemologists
210 Post Street #321
San Francisco, CA  94108
Tel. (415)  781-0063        Kathleen Beaulieu (CGA)

Balzan's Gemological Lab
P.O. Box 6007
San Rafael, CA  94903
Tel. (415)  924-1201        Cortney G. Balzan (MGA)

145

Barrett W. Reese-Goldsmith
499 No. Central Avenue
Upland, CA 91766
Tel. (714) 981-7902                    Barrett W. Reese (CGA)

Brewsters
6052 Magnolia Avenue
Riverside, CA 92506
Tel. (714) 686-1979                    Frank A. Wright

Bubar's Jeweler
Santa Monica Place
Santa Monica, CA 90401
Tel. (213) 451-0727                    Basil Marnoff (CGA)

Cardinal Jewelers
1807-L Santa Rita Road
Pleasanton, CA 94566
Tel. (415) 462-6666                    James A. Kuhn (CGA)

Charles H. Barr Jewelers
1048 Irvine Avenue
Westcliff Plaza
Newport Beach, CA 92660
Tel. (714) 642-3310                    Donna H. Blackman (CGA)

Chase Jewelers, Inc.
20442 Redwood Road
Castro Valley, CA 94546
Tel. (415) 581-0632                    Edward A. Chase (CGA)

Currie & Underwood
3957 Goldfinch Street
San Diego, CA 92103
Tel. (619) 291-8850                    Thom Sorensen Underwood, MGA

Dudenhoeffer Fine Jewelry, Ltd.
118 E. Main Street
El Cajon, CA 92020
Tel. (619) 588-9001                    Roy Dudenhoeffer (CGA)

146

Dudenhoeffer Fine Jewelry, Ltd.
123 Horton Plaza
San Diego, CA  92101
Tel. (619) 236-0316

European Gemological Laboratory
608 S. Hill Street, Ste. 1013
Los Angeles, CA  90014
Tel. (213) 623-8092                          Thomas Tashey (CMA)

Finley-Gracer
5112 E. Second Street
Long Beach, CA  90903
Tel. (213) 434-4429                          Warren Finley (CGA)

Frederic H. Rubel Jewelers
167 Central City Mall
San Bernardino, CA  92401
Tel: (714) 889-9565                          Gary W. Rubel (CGA)

Frederic H. Rubel Jewelers
560 Main Place
2800 N. Main Street
Santa Ana, CA  92701
Tel:  (714) 558-9144                         David A. Rubel (CGA)

The Gem Connection
9227 Haven Avenue
Rancho Cucamonga, CA  91730
Tel: (714) 941-4500                          Ronald L. Base (MGA)

Gem Profiles
416 West Santa Ana
Fresno, CA  93705
Tel: (209) 229-7361                          Bob Praska

George Carter Jessop & Co.
1025 Second Avenue
Westgate Mall
San Diego, CA  92101
Tel: (619) 234-4137                          James C. Jessop (CGA)

147

Gleim the Jeweler
119 Stanford Shopping Center
Palo Alto, CA 94304
Tel: (415) 325-3533        David C. Loudy (CGA)

Grebetus & Son Jewelers
Country Club Centre
3332 El Camino
Sacramento, CA 95821
Tel: (916) 487-7853        Robert Grebitus (CGA)

Grebetus & Son Jewelers
511 L Street
Sacramento, CA 95814
Tel: (916) 442-9081        J. Marlene White (CGA)

G M E
1600 Howe Avenue
Sacramento, CA 95825
Tel: (916) 925-6711        Alison LeBaron (MGA)
G. Marilyn Thomas (MGA)

Hammond's Jewelry, Inc.
16 N. Tower Square
Tulare, CA 93274
Tel: (209) 686-9224        Richard Hammond (CGA)

The Hardware Store, Fine Jewelry
11621 Barrington Court
Los Angeles, CA 90049
Tel: (213) 472-2970        Gary M. Murray (CGA)

Harlequin Jewelry Design
3158 Jefferson Street
Napa, CA 94558
Tel: (707) 255-2121        Mark London (CGA)

Harwin Jewelers
110 S. Hope Avenue
Santa Barbara, CA 93105
Tel: (805) 682-8838        Joel S. Harwin (CGA)

148

Houston Jewelers
4454C Van Nuys Blvd.
Sherman Oaks, CA 91423
Tel: (818) 783-1122                          Richard Houston (CGA)

International Gemological Laboratory
650 Hill Street, Suite 229
Los Angeles, CA 90014
Tel: (213) 688-7837                          Andrew Y. K. Kim (MGA)

J.C. Humphries Jewelers
1835 Newport Blvd. #D152
Costa Mesa, CA 92627
Tel: (714) 548-3401                          Joseph C. Humphries (CGA)

Jack E. Rich Jewelers, Inc.
338 Merchant Street
Vacaville, CA 95688
Tel: (707) 448-4808                          Dale S. Rich (CGA)

Jewels by Stacy
458 Morro Bay Blvd.
Morro Bay, CA 93442
Tel: (805) 772-1003                          Nancey Frey Stacy (MGA)

Johnson & Co. Jewelers
111 Stanford Shopping Center
Palo Alto, CA 94304
Tel: (415) 321-0764                          Steven Graham (CGA)

Johnson Jewelers
16727 S. Bellflower Blvd.
Bellflower, CA 90706
Tel: (213) 867-4420                          Russell Sowell (CGA)

Lee Frank Mfg. Jewelers
2200 Shattuck Avenue
Berkeley, CA 94704
Tel: (415) 843-6410                          Angie Dang (CGA)

Lynn's Jewelry
2434 E. Main Street
Ventura, CA 93003
Tel: (805) 648-4544                          Robert A. Lynn (CGA)

Marshall Adams Gems
2364 N. Del Rosa Avenue #8
San Bernardino, CA 92404
Tel: (714) 883-8463                      Marshall A. Adams (MGA)

Montclair Jewelers
2083 Mountain Blvd.
Oakland, CA 94611
Tel: (415) 339-8547                          David J. Coll (CGA)

Morgan's Jewelers, Inc.
311 Del Amo Fashion Center
Torrance, CA 90503
Tel: (213) 542-5925                        Marshall Varon (CGA)

Morton Jewelers, Inc.
212 N. Santa Cruz Avenue
Los Gatos, CA 95030
Tel: (408) 395-3500                      Sue Maron-Szuks (CGA)

Nielsen Jewelers, Inc.
1581 W. Main Street
Barstow, CA 92311
Tel: (619) 256-3333                        Carl G. Nielsen (CGA)

Norman Mahan Jewelers
2211 Lakspur Landing Circle
Larkspur, CA 94939
Tel: (415) 461-5333                  Nancy Mahan-Weber (CGA)

Robann's Jewelers
125 S. Palm Canyon Drive
Palm Springs, CA 92262
Tel: (619) 325-9603                      Roger Kerchman (CGA)

San Diego Gemological Laboratory
3957 Goldfinch Street
San Diego, CA  92103
Tel: (619)  291-8852                              Thom Underwood (MGA)


Shoemake's Jeweller/Gemologist
1323 J Street
Modesto, CA  95454
Tel: (209)  577-3711                              Otto R. Zimmerman (CGA)


Sidney Mobell Fine Jewelry
141 Post Street
San Francisco, CA  94108
Tel: (415)  421-4747                              Philip Chen (CGA)


Smith Jewelers
704 San Ramon Valley Blvd.
Danville, CA  94526
Tel: (415)  837-3191                   Laurence James Smith (CGA)


Stucki Jewelers
148 Mill Street
Grass Valley, CA  95945
Tel: (916)  272-9618                           George M. Delong (CGA)


Timothy Fidge & Co.
27 Town & Country Village
Palo Alto, CA  94301
Tel: (415)  323-4653                            Patricia Rickard (CGA)


Troy & Company
527 South Lake Avenue, #105
Pasadena, CA  91101
Tel: (818)  449-8414                     Troy B. Steckenrider (CGA)


United States Gemological Services
14080 Yorba Street, #237
Tustin, CA  92680
Tel: (714)  838-8747                              David Ascher

The Village Jeweler
1014-8 Westlake Blvd.
Westlake Village, CA  91361
Tel: (805)  497-4114                                       James W. Coote (CGA)

Wickersham Jewelers
3320 Truxtun Avenue
Bakersfield, CA  93301
Tel: (805)  324-6521                                       John C. Abrams (CGA)

Wight Jewelers
207 N. Euclid Avenue
Ontario, CA  91762
Tel: (714)  984-2745                                       P. Donald Riffe (CGA)

COLORADO

Merritt Sherer, Gemologist
Southmoor Park Center
6448 East Hampden Avenue
Denver, CO  80222
Tel: (303)  691-9414                                       Merritt Sherer (CGA)

Molberg's Jewelers-Gemologist, Inc.
University Hills Shopping Center
2700 S. Colorado Blvd.
Denver, CO  80222
Tel: (303)  757-8325                                  Leonard J. Molberg (CGA)

Purvis Jewelers, Inc.
9797 West Colfax Avenue, #2G
Lakewood, CO  80215
Tel: (303)  233-2798                                       John Purvis III (CGA)

Walters & Hogsett Fine Jewelers
2425 Canyon Blvd.
Boulder, CO  80302
Tel: (303)  449-2626                                       William Lacert (CGA)

Zerbe Jewelers, Inc.
118 N. Tejon Street
Colorado Springs, CO  80903
Tel: (719) 635-3521                                    Charles J. Zerbe (CGA)

CONNECTICUT

Addessi Jewelry Store
207 Main Street
Danbury, CT  06810
Tel: (203) 744-2555                              Doreen A. Guerrera (CGA)

Craig's Jewelry Store
394 Main Street
Ridgefield, CT  06877
Tel: (203) 438-3701                               William D. Craig (CGA)

Lux Bond & Green
        Somerset Square
        Glastonbury, CT  06033
        Tel: (203) 659-8510              Cynthia L. Konney (CGA)
                and at
        15 Pratt Street
        Hartford, CT  06103
        Tel: (203) 278-3050                    John A. Green (CGA)
                and at
        46 La Salle Road
        West Hartford, CT  06107
        Tel: (203) 521-3015                    Marc A. Green (CGA)

M.B.A. Associates
99 Pratt Street
Hartford, CT  06103
Tel: (203) 527-6036                               Neil H. Cohen (MGA)

Michaels Jewelers
127 Bank Street
Waterbury, CT  06702
Tel: (203) 754-5154                                Ernest Bader (CGA)

Michael's Jewelers
926 Chapel Street
New Haven, CT 06510
Tel: (203) 865-6145

Michaels Jewelers, Inc.
80 Main Street
Torrington, CT 06790
Tel: (203) 482-6553                            Edward Bush (CGA)

Neil Cohen Gemologist
99 Pratt Street
Hartford, CT 06103
Tel: (203) 247-1319                            Neil Cohen (MGA)

DELAWARE

Continental Jewelers
1732 Marsh Road
Graylyn Shopping Center
Wilmington, DE 19810
Tel: (302) 478-7190                            Paul S. Cohen (CGA)

FLORIDA

Antares & Co., Gems & Jewelry
5613 University Blvd., W.
Jacksonville, FL 32216
Tel: 904) 737-8316                            B Young McQueen (MGA)

Bechtel Jewelers, Inc.
226 Datura Street
West Palm Beach, FL 33401
Tel: (407) 655-8255                            Robert L. Bechtel (CGA)

Burt's Jewelers
1706 N.E. Miami Gardens Drive
Miami, FL 33179
Tel: (305) 947-8386                            Lloyd Aaron (MGA)

Carroll's Jewelers, Inc.
915 E. Las Olas Blvd.
Ft. Lauderdale, FL 33301
Tel: (305) 463-3711                     Robert B. Moorman, Jr. (CGA)

Gause & Son Oaks Mall
6663 Newberry Road
Gainesville, FL 32605
Tel: (904) 374-4417                     Albert Seelbach (CGA)

Gemological Lab Service Corporation
22 N. W. 1$^{st}$ Street, Suite 101
Miami, FL 33128
Tel: (305) 371-6437                     David M. Levison (MGA)

Gemstone Corporation of America
7507 S. Trail
Sarasota, FL 34231
Tel: (813) 921-4214                     Carol M. Daunt (MGA)
                                        John J. Daunt III (MGA)

Griner's Jewelry Haven, Inc.
850 Cypress Gardens Blvd.
Winter Haven, FL 33880
Tel: (813) 294-4100                     Randall M. Griner (CGA)

Harold Oppenheim (MGA)
633 N.E. 167$^{th}$ Street, Rm.#1023
North Miami Beach, FL 33162
Tel: (305) 652-1319

Independent Gem Testing, Inc.
2455 E. Sunrise Blvd. #501
Fort Lauderdale, FL 33304
Tel: (305) 563-2901                     William C. Horvath (MGA)

J.B. Smith & Son Jewelers, Inc.
900 E. Atlantic Avenue, Suite 21
Delray Beach, FL 33483
Tel: (407) 278-3346                     James T. Smith (CGA)

155

Jaylyn Gemologists Goldsmiths
30 S.E. 4<sup>th</sup> Street
Boca Raton, FL  33432
Tel: (305)  391-0013                                    James O'Sullivan

Joseph W. Tenhagen Gemstones, Inc.
36 NE First Street, Suite 419
Miami, FL  33132
Tel: (305)  374-2411                         Joseph Tenhagen (MGA)

Kempf's Jewelers, Inc.
236 fifth Avenue
Indialantic, FL  32903
Tel: (407)  724-5820                            Gale M. Kempf (CGA)

Lee Jewelry
1823 East Colonial Drive
Orlando, FL  32803
Tel: (407)  896-2566                             Robert A. Lee (CGA)

Mayor's Jewelers, Inc.
283 Catalonia Avenue
Coral Gables, FL  33134
Tel: (305)  442-4233                            Bruce Handler (CGA)

Moon Jewelry Company
536 N. Monroe
Tallahassee, FL  32301
Tel: (804)  224-9000                         Jeff Hofmeister (CGA)

The Oak's Keepsake Diamond Gallery
The Oaks Mall A-13
Gainesville, FL  32605
Tel: (904)  331-5337

P.J. Abramson, Inc.
180 N. Park Avenue, Suite 4D
Winter Park, FL  32789
Tel: (407)  644-3383                    Pamela J. Abramson (CMA)

156

Paul J. Schmmitt Jeweler
765 Fifth Avenue S.
Naples, FL  33940
Tel: (813)  262-4251                    Paul J. Schmitt (CGA)

Paul J. Schmitt Jeweler
4321 Tamiami Trail
Naples, FL  33940
Tel: (813)  261-0600                    James T. Merkley (CGA)

Peter Bradley, Inc.
13499 US 41 S.E.
Fort Myers, FL  33907
Tel: (813)  482-7550                    Peter F. Bradley (MGA)

Roger Hunt & Son
Division Maison D'Or Inc.
232 S.W. 10<sup>th</sup> Street
Ocala, FL  32671
Tel: (904)  629-1105                    Roger E. Hunt (CGA)

Suncoast Accredited Gem. Laboratory
Bayshore Office Bldg.
6221 14<sup>th</sup> Street West, Suite 105
Bradenton, FL  34207
Tel: (813)  756-8787

Wells Jewelers, Inc.
4452 Hendricks Avenue
Jacksonville, FL  32207
Tel: (904)  730-0111                    Laurence Bodkin (CGA)

GEORGIA

Ford, Gittings & Kane, Inc.
312 Broad Street
Rome, GA  30161
Tel: (404)  291-8811                    Jan J. Fergerson (CGA)

HAWAII

Hallmark Jewelers
2242 Ala Moana Center
Oahu, Honolulu
Hawaii 96814
Tel: (808) 949-3982                    Yoshimasa Ishihara (CGA)

ILLINOIS

Denney Jewelers
51 Central Park Plaza South
Jacksonville, IL 62650
Tel: (217) 245-4718                    Shane S. Denney (CGA)

Doerner Jewelers
9201 North Milwaukee Avenue
Niles, IL 60648
Tel: (312) 966-1341                    Michael Doerner (CGA)

Fey & Company Jewelers, Inc.
1156 Fox Valley Center
Aurora, IL 60505
Tel: (312) 851-8828                    Edgard H. Fey III (CGA)

Franz Jewelers, Ltd.
1220 Meadow Road
Northbrook, IL 60062
Tel: (312) 272-4100                    Frank E. Pintz (CGA)

Rand Jewelers, Inc.
2523A Waukegan Road
Bannockburn Green Shopping Center
Bannockburn, IL 60015
Tel: (312) 948-9475                    William E. Rand (CGA)

Samuels Jewelers, Inc.
4500 16th Street
South Park Mall
Moline, IL 61265
Tel: (309) 762-9375                    Corey James England (CGA)

Stout and Lauer
1650 Wabash The Yard
Springfield, IL 62704
Tel: (217) 793-3040                    Deborah Lauer-Toelle (CGA)

INDIANA

Droste's Jewelry Shoppe, Inc.
4511 First Avenue
Evansville, IN 47710
Tel: (812) 422-4351                    Gregory Scott Droste (CGA)

Philip E. Nelson Jeweler, Inc.
22 E. Main Street
Brownsburg, IN 46112
Tel: (317) 852-2306                    Jeffrey R. Nelson (CGA)

Troxel Jewelers, Inc.
7980 Broadway
Merrilville, IN 46410
Tel: (219) 769-0770                    Donald Troxel (CGA)

Williams Jewelry, Inc.
114 N. Walnut
Bloomington, IN 47408
Tel: (812) 339-2231                    Mark A. Thomas (CGA)

IOWA

Becker's Jewelers
123 West Monroe
Mt. Pleasant, IA 52641
Tel: (319) 385-3722                    William D. Becker (CGA)

Gunderson's Jewelers
Terra Center
600 Fourth Street
Sioux City, IA 51101
Tel: (712) 255-7229                    Brian Gunderson (CGA)

Josephs Jewelers
320 6<sup>th</sup> Avenue
Des Moines, IA 50309
Tel: (515) 283-1961                    William J. Baum (CGA)

Mark Ginsberg (MGA)
110 E. Washington Street
Iowa City, IA 52240
Tel: (319) 351-1700

Samuel's Jewelers, Inc.
320 W. Kimberly
North Park Mall
Davenport, IA 52806
Tel: (319) 391-4362                    Peggy K. Friedericks (CGA)

Thorpe & Company Jewellers
501 4<sup>th</sup> Street
Sioux City, IA 51101
Tel: (712) 258-7501                    Bruce C. Anderson (CGA)

KANSAS

Donaldson's Jewelers, Inc.
Seabrook Center
2001 S.W. Gage Blvd.
Topeka, KS 66604
Tel: (913) 273-5080                    Tracie E. Forkner (CGA)

Jewelry Arts, Inc.
8221 Corinth Square
Prairie Village, KS 66208
Tel: (913) 381-8444                    Ryudy Giessenbier (CGA)

Lavery's Jewelry
404 Delaware
Leavenworth, KS 66048
Tel: (913) 682-3182                          Evelyn J. Chapman  (CGA)

Riley's Jewelry, Inc.
6116 Johnson Drive
Mission, KS 66202
Tel: (913) 432-8484                          William A. Riley (CGA)

KENTUCKY

Bernard Lewis & Company
313 Broadway
Paducah,KY 42001
Tel: (502) 442-0002, (800) 327-4056          Bernard G. Lewis (CGA)

Brundage Jewelers
141 Chenoweth Lane
Louisville, KY 40207
Tel: (502) 895-7717                          William E. Brundage (CGA)

Cortland Hall Jewelers, Inc.
133 St. Matthews Avenue
Louisville, KY 40207
Tel: (502) 897-6024                          Mark L. Redmon (CGA)

Farmer's Jewelry
821 Euclid Avenue
Lexington, KY 40502
Tel: (606) 266-6241                          William L. Farmer (CGA)

Merkley Jewelers
400 Old East Vine
Lexinton, KY 40507
Tel: (606) 254-1548                          Kimberley S. Hall (CGA)

Merkley-Kendrick Jewelers, Inc.
138 Chenoweth Lane
Louisville, KY 40207
Tel: (502) 895-6124                    Donald J. Merkley (CGA)

Miller & Woodward, Inc.
115 West Short Street
Lexington, KY 40507
Tel: (606) 233-3001                    Russell Pattie (CGA)

Seng Jewelers
453 Fourth Avenue
Louisville, KY 40202
Tel: (502) 585-5109                    Lee S. Davis (CGA)

LOUISIANA

Champion Jewelers -- Gemologists
1123 North Pine Street
Park Terrace Shopping Center
De Ridder, LA 70634
Tel: (318) 463-7026                    John Cunningham (CGA)

Clarkes Jewelers, Inc.
3916 Youree Drive
Shreveport, LA 71105
Tel: (318) 865-5568                    Gary L. Clarke (CGA)

Simon Jeweller Gemmologist, Inc.
941 E. 70th Street
Shreveport, LA 71106                   Horace Simon (CGA)

MAINE

Browne Goldsmiths & Co., Inc.
One Mechanic Street
Freeport, ME 04032
Tel: (207) 865-4126                    W. Stephen Brown (CGA)

Etienne & Company
20 Main Street
Camden, ME 04843
Tel: (207) 236-9696, (800) 426-4367          Peter Theriault (CGA)

J. Dostie Jeweler
4 Lisbon Street
Lewiston, ME 04240
Tel: (207) 782-7758          Linda Chamberlain (CGA)

MARYLAND

Colonial Jewelry, Inc.
9 W. Patrick Street, PO Box 674
Frederick, MD 21701
Tel: (301) 663-9252          Jeffrey I. Hurwitz (MGA)

National Gem Appraising Laboratory
8600 Fenton Street
Silver Spring, MD 20910          Antonio C. Bonnano (MGA)
          Karen J. Ford (MGA)

Tilghman Company
44 State Circle
Annapolis, MD 21401
Tel: (301) 268-7855          Thomas O. Tilghman (CGA)

MASSACHUSETTS

Andrew Grant Diamond Center
144 Elm Street
Westfield, MA 01805
Tel: (413) 562-2432          Robert K. Grant (CGA)

Appraisal Associates
7 Kent Street
Brookline Village, MA 02146
Tel: (617) 566-1339          Nancy A. Smith (MGA)

Kenyon A.Carr Jeweler
422 Main Street
Hyannis, MA  02601
Tel: (617)  775-1968                    William F. Carr (CGA)

La France Jeweler
763 Purchase Street
New Bedford, MA  02740
Tel: (508)  993-1137                    Paul R. Rousseau (CGA)

Sharfmans, Inc.
164 Worcester Center
Worcester, MA  01608
Tel: (508)  791-2211, (800)  451-7500
Nancy R. Rosenberg (CGA)

Shreve, Crump & Low
330 Boylston Street
Boston, MA  02116                       Joseph P. Pyne (CGA)

Swanson Jeweler, Inc.
717 Massachusetts Avenue
Arlington, MA  02174
Tel: (617)  643-4209                    Robert Swanson (CGA)

MICHIGAN

Birmingham Gemological Services
251 Merrill Street
Birmingham, MI  48011
Tel: (313)  644-8828                    James Krol (CMA)

Dobie Jewelers
        14600 Lakeside Circle #205
        Lakeside Mall
        Sterling Heights, MI  48078
        Tel: (313)  247-1730            Edmund P. Dery (CGA)
                and at

500 S. Washington Street
Royal Oak, MI 48067
Tel: (313) 545-8400                    Joseph M. Cayuela (CGA)

Everts Jewelers, Inc.
109 E. Broadway
Mount Pleasant, MI 48858
Tel: (517) 772-3141                    Lawrence W. Everts (CGA)

F.A. Earl Jewelers
156 E. Front Street
Traverse City, MI 49684
Tel: (616) 947-7602                    Brad Shepler  (CGA)

Haffner Jewelers
3204 Rochester Road
Royal Oak, MI 48073
Tel: (313) 588-6622                    David Williamson (MGA)

J.F. Reusch Jewlers
427 E. Mitchell Street
Petoskey, MI 49770
Tel: (616) 347-2403                    John F. Reusch (CGA)

Jules R. Schubot Jewellers
3001 W. Big Beaver Rd., #112
Troy, MI 48084
Tel: (313) 649-1122                    Brian T. Schubot (CGA)

Losey's Fine Jewelry
133 East Main Street
Midland, MI 48640
Tel: (517) 631-1143                    Roger E. Schmidt (CGA)

Milkins Jewelers, Inc.
13 Washington Street
Monroe, MI 48161
Tel: (313) 242-1023                    Bruce A. Milkins (CGA)

Mosher's Jewelers, Inc.
336 Huron Avenue
Port Huron, MI 48060
Tel: (313) 987-2768                    William A. Mosher (CGA)

Siegel Jewelers
        Amway Grand Plaza Hotel
        Pearl & Monroe
        Grand Rapids, MI 49503
        Tel: (616) 459-7263            B. Miller Siegel (CGA)
              and at
        28 Woodland Mall
        3135 28$^{th}$ S.E.
        Grand Rapids, MI 49508
        Tel: (616) 949-7370            James W. Siegel (CGA)

MINNESOTA

Bockstruck Jewelers
27 W. Fifth Street
St. Paul, MN 55102
Tel: (612) 222-1858                    DeWayne Amundsen (CGA)

Korst & Sons Jewelers
3901 W. 50$^{th}$ Street
Edina, MN 55424
Tel: (612) 926-0303                    William Korst, Jr. (CGA)

R.F. Moeller Jeweler
2073 Ford Parkway
St. Paul, MN 55116
Tel: (612) 698-6321                    Mark Moeller (CGA)

Stadheim Jewelers
215 S. Broadway
Albert Lea, MN 56007
Tel: (507) 373-3440                    Beth S. Ordalen (CGA)

MISSISSIPPI

Way-Fil Jewelry
1123 W. Main Street
Tupelo, MS 38801
Tel: (601) 844-2427                              Patricia A. Witt (CGA)

MISSOURI

Clayton Gemological Services, Inc.
Bemiston Tower, Suite 800
231 South Bemiston
St. Louis, MO 63105-1914
Tel: (314) 862-4005                              Therese S. Kienstra

Elleard B. Heffern, Inc.
7777 Bonhomme Avenue, Suite 1800
St. Louis, MO 63105
Tel: (314) 863-8820                              Christopher E. Heffern (CGA)

Frank Gooden Co., Inc. Gemlab
1110 Grand Avenue
Kansas City, MO 64106
Tel: (816) 421-0281                              Ricki Kendall Gooden

Tivol, Inc.
220 Nichols Road
Kansas City, MO 64112
Tel: (816) 531-5800                              J. Michael Tracy (CGA)

MONTANA

Black's Jewelers
211 Third Avenue Box 869
Havre, MT 59501
Tel: (406) 265-2522, (800) 843-3564    Richard J. Growney (CGA)

Chaussee Precious Gems & Fine Jewelry
228 N. Higgins
Missoula, MT 59802
Tel: (406) 728-8639                    Yvette I. Clevish (CGA)

Crown Jewelry, Inc.
419 Central Avenue
Great Falls, MT 59401
Tel: (406) 453-5312                    E.W. O'Neill (CGA)

NEBRASKA

Karl's Jewelry
84 West 6th, Box 710
Fremont, NB 68025
Tel: (402) 721-1727                    Karl Rasmussen IV (CGA)

Michael's Jewelry of Fremont, N.E. Inc.
540 N. Main Street
Fremont, NB 68025
Tel: (402) 721-7300                    Dolores Dunker (CGA)

Sartor-Hamann Jewelers
         3404 W. 13th Street
         Grand Island, NB 68803
         Tel: (308) 382-5850           Bennett Murphy, Jr. (CGA)
                  and at
         11150 "O" Street
         Lincoln, NB 68508
         Tel: (402) 226-2917           Robert H. Fixer (CGA)

NEVADA

Huntington Jewelers, Inc.
3661 S. Maryland Parkway #19N
Las Vegas, NV 89109
Tel: (702) 732-1977                    Richard C.Huntington (MGA)

NEW HAMPSHIRE

A.E. Alie & Sons, Inc.
1 Market Street
Portsmouth, NH 03801
Tel: (603) 436-0531                              Stephen R. Alie (CGA)

Beacon Hill Jewelers, Inc.
42 Hanover Street
Manchester, NH 03101
Tel: (603) 627-7338                              Judith Fineblit (CGA)

Harrington's Jewelers
        New London Shopping Center
        New London, NH 03257
        Tel: (603) 526-4440                      Douglas J. Lantz (CGA)
                and at
        33 Main Street
        Newport, NH 036773
        Tel: (603) 863-1662                      Douglas J. Lantz (CGA)

Sawyers Jewelry
Downtown Laconia Mall
Laconia, NH 03246
Tel: (603) 524-3309                              Richard Beauregard (CGA)

NEW JERSEY

Earth Treasures
Circle Plaza Shopping Center
Eatontown, NJ 07724
Tel: (201) 542-5444                              Paul Bischoff
Hamilton Jewelers
2542 Brunswick Pike
Lawrenceville, NJ 08648
Tel: (609) 771-9400                              Hank B. Siegel (CGA)

The Jewel Shop
436 Main Street
Metuchen, NJ 08840
Tel: (201) 549-1490                              Andrew H. Zagoren (CGA)

Martin Jewelers
     12 North Avenue West
     Cranford, NJ 07016
     Tel: (201) 276-6718         Ellen R. Ramer (CGA)
          and at
     125 Quimby Street
     Westfield, NJ 07090
     Tel: (201) 232-6718       Davia Sue Freeman (CGA)

Rose City Jewelers-Gemologists
Corner of Waverly & Main Street
Madison, NJ 07940
Tel: (201) 377-2146         Joseph Falco, Jr. (CGA)

Simms Jewelers, Inc.
17 Mine Brook Road
Bernardsville, NJ 07924
Tel: (201) 766-4455         Arthur Sockolof (CGA)

NEW MEXICO

Butterfield Personal Service Jewelers
2411 San Pedro, N.E.
Albuquerque, NM 87110
Tel: (505) 884-5747         Larry D. Phillips (CGA)

J.A. May Jewelers, Inc.
112 West Main Street
Farmington, NM 87401
Tel: (505) 325-5102         William D. McGraw, (CGA)

Larry D. Phillips (MGA)
801 Marie Park NE
Albuquerque, NM 87123
Tel: (505) 884-5747

Shelton Jewelers, Ltd.
7001 Montgomery Blvd., N.E.
Albuquerque, NM 87109
Tel: (505) 881-1013                    Eric M. Shelton (CGA)

NEW YORK

American Gemological Laboratory
580 Fifth Avenue,Suite 1211
New York, NY 10036
Tel: (212) 704-0727                    C.R. "Cap" Beesley (MGA)

Castiglione Gem Jewelers Inc.
25 N. Main Street
Gloversville, NY 12078
Tel: (518) 725-1113                    Louis J. Castiglione (CGA)

Cornell Jewelers
          Dutchess Mall, Rt. 9
          Fishkill, NY 12524
          Tel: (914) 896-8950          Thomas F. Kavanagh (CGA)
                and at
          119 Newburgh Mall
          1067 Union Avenue
          Newburgh/Beacon, NY 12550
          Tel: (914) 564-5100          Charles T. Kavanagh (CGA)

Freedman Jewelers
345 New York Avenue
Huntington, NY 11743
Tel: (516) 423-2000                    Eric M. Freedman (CGA)

Lights Jewelers & Gemologists
Plattsburgh Plaza
Plattsburgh, NY 12901
Tel: (518) 561-6623                    Andre Thomas Light (CGA)

Lourdes Gemological Laboratory
Rt. 6 & Hill Blvd.
Jefferson Valley, NY  10535
Tel: (914)  245-4676                          Howard N. Biffer (MGA)

Reyman Jewelers, Inc.
16 W. First Street
Mount Venon, NY  10550
Tel: (914)  668-9281                          Mark Reyman (CGA)

Ruby & Sons Jewelers
6 Washington Avenue
Endicott, NY  13760
Tel: (607)  754-1212                          Leonard Levine (CGA)

Schneider's Jewelers, Inc.
290 Wall Street
Kingston, NY  12401
Tel: (914)  331-1888                          Thomas W. Jacobi (CGA)

T.H. Bolton Jeweler, Inc.
16 East Main Street
Rochester, NY  14614
Tel: (716)  546-7074                          E. Jean Bolton (CGA)

Van Cott Fine Jewelry
Oakdale Mall
Johnson City, NY  13790
Tel: (607)  729-9108

William Scheer Jewelers, Inc.
3349 Monroe Avenue, Pittsford Plaza
Rochester, NY  14618
Tel: (716)  381-3050                          Jack Monchecourt (CGA)

NORTH CAROLINA

Arnold Jewelers
305 Overstreet Mall
Southern National Center
Charlotte, NC 28202
Tel: (704) 332-6727                                    Frank V. Taylor (CGA)

Bailey's Fine Jewelry
117 Winstead Avenue
Rocky Mount, NC 27804
Tel: (919) 443-7676, (800) 338-7676                    Clyde Bailey (CGA)

Green's Jewelers
106 N. Main Street
Roxboro, NC 27573
Tel: (919) 599-8381                                    Sam B. Green (CGA)

Henry J. Young's Diamonds and Fine Jewelry
257 N. Hills Mall
Raleigh, NC 27609
Tel: (919) 787-1422                                    Henry J. Young (CGA)

Johnson's Jewelers, Inc.
309 Fayetteville Street
Raleigh, NC 27602
Tel: (919) 834-0713

Karat Gold Corner, Inc.
1809 Pembroke Road
Greensboro, NC 27408
Tel: (919) 272-2325                                    Lorraine D. Dodds (CGA)

McCormick Jewelers
        9015-1 J.M. Keynes Drive
        Charlotte, NC 28213
        Tel: (704) 547-8446                            Jame G. McCormick (CGA)
        and at

3716 MacCorkle Avenue, S.E.
Charleston, WV 25304
Tel: (304) 925-3435                    James R. McCormick (CGA)


NC Gem Lab
107 Hunter's Ridge Road
Chapel Hill, NC 27514
Tel: (919) 966-2227                    William Benedick (MGA)


Parker-Miller Jewelers
100 S. Main Street
Lexington, NC 27292
Tel: (704) 249-8174                    Christopher L. Bramlett (CGA)


T. William Benedict (MGA)
107 Hunter Ridge Road
Chapel Hill, NC 27514
Tel: (919) 929-9179


Wick & Greene Jewelers
121 Patton Avenue
Asheville, NC 28801
Tel: (704) 253-1805                    Michael E. Greene (CGA)


OHIO


Argo & Lehne Jewelers
20 S. Third Street
Columbus, OH 43215
Tel: (614) 228-6338                    Shannon F. Patterson (CGA)


David Baker Creative Jewelers, Inc.
37 West Bridge Street
Dublin, OH 43017
Tel: (614) 764-0068                    David M. Baker (CGA)


E.M. Smith Jewelers, Inc.
668 Central Center
Chillicote, OH 45601
Tel: (614) 774-1840                    Robert J. Smith (CGA)

Grassmuck & Lange Jewelers, Inc.
441 Vine Street
Carew Tower Arcade
Cincinnati, OH 45202
Tel: (513) 621-1898                    William F. Grassmuck  (CGA)

Henry B. Ball
        2291 W. Market Street
        Pilgrim Square
        Akron, OH  44313
        Tel: (216)  867-9800           Mary Ball Gorman (CGA)
                and at
        5254 Dressler Road, N.W.
        Belden Village
        Canton, OH  44718
        Tel: (216)  499-3000                Robert A. Ball (CGA)

Jack Siebert, Goldsmith & Jeweler
1623 W. Lane Avenue Center
Columbus, OH  43221
Tel: (614) 486-4653                         Jack Siebert (CGA)

John Gasser & Son Jewelers
205 Third Street, N.W.
Canton, OH  44702
Tel: (216) 452-3204                    Gerald D. Blevins (CGA)

O'Bryant Jewelers & Gemologist
101 E. Wayne Street
Maumee, OH  43537
Tel: (419)  893-9771                  James P. O'Bryant (CGA)

Raymond Brenner, Inc.
7081 West Blvd., Route 224
Youngstown, OH  44512
Tel: (216)  726-8816                Raymond Brenner, Jr. (CGA)

Thomas Jewelers, Inc.
409 S. Main Street
Findlay, OH 45840
Tel: (419) 422-3775                    James L. Thomas (CGA)

Wendel's
137 S. Broad Street
Lancaster, OH 43130
Tel: (614) 653-6402                    Stuart Palestrant (CGA)

William Effler Jewelers
7618 Hamilton Avenue
Cincinnati, OH 45231
Tel: (513) 521-6654                    Mark T. Andrus (CGA)

Yaeger Jewelers, Inc.
14814 Madison Avenue
Lakewood, OH 44107
Tel: (216) 521-6658                    Jack Yaeger (CGA)

OKLAHOMA

B.C. Clark, Inc.
101 Park Avenue
Oklahoma City, OK 73102
Tel: (405) 232-8806                    Paul C. Minton (CGA)

OREGON

Deuell Jewelers, Inc.
1327 Main Street
Philomath, OR 97370
Tel: (503) 929-3422                    JoAnne Hansen (CGA)

Gayer Jewelers
300 E. Second Street
The Dalles, OR 97058
Tel: (503) 298-GEMS                    Scott Gayer (CGA)

The Gem Lab
20776 St. George Court
Bend, OR 97702
Tel: (503) 389-6790                    Jim "Fritz" Ferguson

Hart Jewelers
235 S.E. 6<sup>th</sup> Street
Grants Pass, OR 97526
Tel: (503) 476-5543                    Thomas R. Hart Sr. (CGA)

PENNSYLVANIA

Bill Lieberum Fine Jewelers & Gemologists
Centre Pointe Place Shopping Center
872 West Street Road
Warminster, PA 18974
Tel: (215) 443-8000                    William R. Lieberum (CGA)

D.A. Palmierie Co., Inc.
666 Washington Road
Pittsburgh, PA 15228
Tel: (412) 344-0300                    Susan G. Bower (MGA)
                                       Donald Palmieri (MGA)

D Atlas & Co. Inc.
732 Sansom Street
Philadelphia, PA 19106
Tel: (215) 922-1926                    Michael Jordan (MGA)
                              Edward R. Skinner, Jr. (MGA)

David Craig Jewelers, Ltd.
Summit Square Shopping Center
Langhorne, PA 19047
Tel: (215) 968-8900                    David C. Rotenberg (CGA)

Futer Bros. Jewelers
Continental Square
York, PA 17401
Tel: (717) 845-2734                    J.H. Eigenrauch III (CGA)

Gemological Appraisal Associates, Inc.
666 Washington Road
Pittsburgh, PA 15228
Tel: (412) 344-5500                    Donald Palmieri (MGA)

John M. Roberts & Sons Co.
429-431 Wood Street
Pittsburgh, PA 15222
Tel: (412) 281-1651                    Maureen F. O'Brien (CGA)

Joseph A. Rosi Jewelers
4636 Jonestown Road
Harrisburg, PA 17109
Tel: (717) 652-8477                    Joseph A. Rosi Jr. (CGA)

M.A.B. Jewelers
1162 Baltimore Pike
Olde Sproul Village
Springfield, PA 19064
Tel: (215) 554-4656                    Samuel S. Bruner (CGA)

N.B. Levy's
120 Wyoming Avenue
Scranton, PA 18503
Tel: (717) 344-6187                    Seymour H. Biederman (CGA)

Yardley Jewelers
JBD Studio - 2 South Main Street
Yardley, PA 19067
Tel: (215) 493-1300                    Jon Barry DiNola (CGA)

RHODE ISLAND

Tilden Thurber Corporation
292 Westminster Street
Providence, RI 02903
Tel: (401) 421-8400                    Robert Quinn (CGA)

## SOUTH CAROLINA

Cochran Jewelry Company of Greenville, Inc.
211 North Main Street
Greenville, SC  29601
Tel: (803) 233-3641                              Walter S. Morris (CGA)

## TENNESSEE

Alexander & Co. Inc.
5050 Poplar, #634
Memphis, TN  38157
Tel: (901)  767-4367                            William A. Mathis (MGA)

Fischer Evans Jewelers
801 Market Street
Chattanooga, TN  37402
Tel: (615)  267-0901                       Mrs. Taylor M. Watson  (CGA)

Helm's Jewelry
100 W. 7$^{th}$ Street
Columbia, TN  38401
Tel: (615)  388-7842                         Debbie Nelson Wells (CGA)

M.M. Schenck Jewelers, Inc.
3953 Hixson Pike
Chattanooga, TN  37415
Tel: (615)  877-4011                        Mrs. Mary Schenck (CGA)

Mackley & Co. Inc.
8906 Kingston Pike, Suite 214
Knoxville, TN  37923
Tel: (615)  693-3097                           Joseph Mackley (MGA)
                                               Emily White Ware (CGA)

Sites Jewelers, Inc.
206 Franklin Street
Clarkesville, TN  37040
Tel: (615)  648-0678                          William C. Sites (CGA)

179

TEXAS

Ann Hawken Gem Laboratory
603 West 13th, Suite 312
Austin, TX 78701
Tel: (512) 288-3590                                        Ann Hawken

Anna M. Miller (MGA)
PO Box 1844
Pearland, TX 77588
Tel: (713) 485-1606

Antique Appraisal Service
PO Box 27903
Houston, TX 77227
Tel: (713) 665-8245                           Christine W. York (MGA)

Barnes Jewelry, Inc.
2611 Wolflin Village
Amarillo, TX 79109
Tel: (806) 355-9874                              Vess Barnes Jr. (CGA)

C. Kirk Root Design
6418 B Westside Drive
Austin, TX 78731
Tel: (512) 338-0360                             Charles K. Root (MGA)

Crowell Jewelers, Inc.
2417 West Park Row
Arlington, TX 76013
Tel : (817) 460-1962                            C.G. Crowell, Jr. (CGA)

Duncan & Boyd, Jewelers
113 West 8th Street
Amarillo, TX 79101
Tel: (806) 373-1067                               Ronald Boyd (CGA)

I. David Clark & Associates
305 21st Street
Galveston, TX 77551
Tel: (409) 762-3229                                   Irving D. Clark (CGA)

Jewelry Forest
9100 N. Central/Park Lane
185 Caruth Plaza
Dallas, TX 75231
Tel: (214) 368 5352                                   Jerry Forest (CGA)

Lacy & Company
River Oakes Shopping Village
3301 South 14th
Abilene, TX 79605
Tel: (915) 695-4700                                   Ellen W. Lacy (CGA)

UTAH

John's Jewelry
3920 Washington Blvd.
Ogden, UT 84403
Tel: (801) 627-0440                                   John Christainsen (CGA)

Robert L. Rosenblatt
2736 Commonwealth Avenue
Salt Lake City, UT 84109
Tel: (801) 364-3667

Spectrum Gems
1615 S. Foothill Drive
Salt Lake City, UT 84108-2742
Tel: (801) 266-4579                                   Dana Lynn Richardson (MGA)

Sutton's of Park City
Park City Resort Village
Park City, UT 84060
Tel: (801) 649-1187                                   Keith M. Sutton (CGA)

VIRGINIA

Carreras, Ltd.
150 Sovran Plaza
Richmond, VA 23277
Tel: (804) 780-9191                     Mark A. Smith (CGA)

Cowardin Jewelers
Chesterfield Towne Center
Rt. 60 and Rt. 147
Richmond, VA 23235
Tel: (804) 794-4478                     Ronald L. Cowardin (CGA)

Everhart Jewelers, Inc.
6649 Old Dominion Drive
McLean, VA 22101
Tel: (703) 821-3344                     William Everhart II (CGA)

Fauquier Gemological Laboratory
PO Box 525, Main Street
Marshall, VA 22115
Tel: (703) 364-1959                     Jelks H. Cabaniss (MGA)

Frank L. Moose Jeweler
207 1st Street S.W.
Roanoke, VA 24011
Tel: (703) 345-8881                     F. Geoffrey Jennings (CGA)

The Greenhouse
PO Box 525
Marshall, VA 22115
Tel: (703) 364-1959                     Jelks Cabaniss (MGA)

Hardy's Diamonds
4212 Virginia Beach Blvd.
Wayside Village, VA 23452
Tel: (804) 486-0469                     George B. Hardy (CGA)

Marvin D. Miller Gemologists
3050 Covington Street
Fairfax, VA 22031
Tel: (703) 280-2169            Marvin D. Miller (MGA)

Schwarzchild Jewelers, Inc.
Broad at Second Street
Richmond, VA 23219
Tel: (804) 644-1941            B Harton Wolf (CGA)

Thomas P. Harnett (MGA)
11344 Links Drive
Reston, VA 22090
Tel: (703) 437-7108

Van Doren Jewelers
6025-D Burke Center Parkway
Burke, VA 22015
Tel: (703) 978-2211        Christian W. Lietwiler (MGA)

## WASHINGTON

Ben Bridge Jeweler
     1101 Pike
     Seattle, WA 98111
     Tel: (206) 628-6879        Jane Ann Nuescher (CGA)
     and at
     1119 Tacoma Mall
     Tacoma, WA 98409
     Tel: (206) 473-1227          Cathy Hall (CGA)

Blessing Jewelers
225 W. Meeker Street
Kent, WA 98032
Tel: (206) 852-3455        Leslie S. Thomas (CGA)

Button Jewelers, Inc.
2 S. Wenatchee Avenue
Wenatchee, WA 98801
Tel: (509) 663-4654                          Douglas D. Button (CGA)

Carroll's Fine Jewelry
1427 Fourth Avenue
Seattle, WA 98101
Tel: (206) 622-9191                          Patricia M. Droge (CGA)

Fox's Gem Shop
1341 Fifth Avenue
Seattle, WA 98101
Tel: (206) 623-2528                          Sandra L. Ordway (CGA)

Gemological Training Corporation
1425 4th Avenue, Suite 502
Seattle, WA 98101
Tel: (206) 625-0105                          David W. Hall (MGA)

Henry Gerards Jewelers, Inc.
W. 714 Main
River Park Square Skywalk
Spokane, WA 99201
Tel: (509) 456-8098                          Janis Ann Gerards (CGA)

Pavilion Gemological Laboratories
19415 Pacific Highway, So. Suite 414
Seattle, WA 98188
Tel: (206) 824-9132                          Joseph V. Paul (MGA)

S.O. Hawkes & Son Jewelers, Inc.
123 E. Yakima Avenue
Yakima, WA 98901
Tel: (509) 248-2248                          Kathy Hawkes Smith (CGA)

WEST VIRGINIA

Calvin Broyles Jewelers
48333 McCorkle Avenue S.W.
Spring Hill, WV 25309
Tel: (304) 768-8821                         Don C. Broyles (CGA)

McCormick Jewelers, Inc.
3716 MacCorkle Avenue, S.E.
Charleston, WV 25304
Tel: (304) 925-3435                  James R. McCormick (CGA)

R.D. Buttermore & Son
623 Market Street
Parkersburg, WV 26101
Tel: (304) 422-6401                   R.D. Buttermore Jr. (CGA)

WISCONSIN

Gemstone Goldsmiths
100 Main Street
Stone Lake, WI 54876
Tel: (715) 865-2422                      David R. Neilson (CGA)

J. Vander Zanden & Sons, Ltd.
217 N. Washington Street
Greenbay, WI 54305
Tel: (414) 432-3155               Peter Vander Zanden (CGA)

Midwest Gem Lab of Wisconsin, Inc.
1335 S. Moorland Road
Brookfield, WI 53005
Tel: (414) 784-9017                     James S. Seaman (MGA)

Rasmussen Jewelry
3119 Washington Avenue
Racine, WI 53405
Tel: (414) 633-9474               William E. Sustachek (CGA)

Schwanke-Kasten Co.
324 E. Silver Spring Drive
Milwaukee, WI 53217
Tel: (414) 964-1242                    James E. Brown (CGA)

WYOMING

Wiseman Jewelers
501 Ivinson Avenue
Laramie, WY 82070
Tel: (307) 745-5240                    Scott Alan Wiseman (CGA)

# APPENDIX E

## INTERNATIONAL DIRECTORY OF GEMOLOGICAL ASSOCIATIONS

### UNITED STATES AND CANADA

Accredited Gemologists Assoc.
1615 South Foothill Drive
Salt Lake City, Utah 84108
801-581-90000 or 364-3667
Dana Richardson, Editor

American Gem Trade Association
#181 World Trade Center
2050 Stemmons Expressway
Dallas, Texas 75207
214-742-4367, 800-972-1162
Peggy Willett, Exec. Director

Appraisers Association of America
60 East 42$^{nd}$ St.
New York, NY 10165
212-867-9775
Victor Wiener, Exec. Director

Association Professionelle des Gemmologists du Quebec
6079, Boul. Monk
Montreal, Quebec, Canada H4E 3H5
514-766-7327

Canadian Gemmological Association
P.O. Box 1106, Station Q
Toronto, Ontario, Canada M4T 2P2
Warren Boyd
416-652-3137

Canadian Jewellers Institute
Canada Trust Tower, Suite 1203
20 Eglinton Ave. W., Box 2021
Toronto, Ontario, Canada M4R 1K8
416-480-1424

Diamond Council of America, Inc.
9140 Ward Parkway
Kansas City, MO 64114
816-444-3500
Jerry Fogel, Executive Director

Diamond Dealers Club, Inc.
580 5th Avenue
New York, NY 10036
212-719-4321
Abe Shainberg, Exec. Director

International Colored Gemstone Association
22643 Strathern St.
West Hills, CA 91304
818-716-0489
Maureen Jones, Exec. Director

Jewelers of America, Inc.
1271 Avenue of the Americas
New York, NY 10020
212-489-0023
Michael D. Roman, Chairman and Exec. Director

National Association of Jewelry Appraisers
4210 North Brown Avenue, Suite "A"
Scottsdale, AZ 85251
602-941-8088
Richard E. Baron, Executive Director

### AUSTRIA

Bundesgremium Des Handels Mit Juwelen
P.O. Box 440
A-1045 Vienna, Austria
Karl M. Heldwein

## AUSTRALIA

Gemmological Association of Australia
P.O. Box m184
East Brisbane, Queensland 4169, Australia

Gemmological Association of Australia
        P.O. Box 104, Bondi Beach
        New South Wales, Australia
        Joy Clayton
                also at
        G.P.O. Box 5133 AA
        Melbourne, 3001 Australia
        Mr. Franz Trhipp

## BRAZIL

ABGM
Rue Barao de Itapetininga
No. 255 - 12 Andar
CEP 01042 - Sau Paulo - SP, Brazil

Ajorio - Sindicato National
Do. Com. Atacadista de Pedras Preciosas
Av. Graca Aranha, 19/40 Andar Sala 404
CEP 20031, Brazil

Associacao Brasileria de Gemologiae
Mineralogiae Rue Alvarez, Machado
41, 18000/801 501
Sao Paulo, Brazil

IBGM
Rua Teixeira Da Silva No. 654
CEP 04002 - Paraiso
Sao Paulo - SP, Brasil

## BURMA

Gem & Jade Corporation
86, Kala Aye Pagoda Road
P.O. Box 1397 Rangoon

## DUBAI

Institute of Goldsmithing & Jewellery
Sikat Al Khail Road, P.O. Box 11489
Duabi, U.A.E.

## ENGLAND

De Beers Consolidated Mines Ltd.
40 Holborn Viaduct
London ECIPIAJ

Gemmological Association of Great Britain
Saint Dunstan's House
Carey Lane
London, EC2V 8AB

Jewellery Information Centre
44 Fleet Street
London, ECA

## FINLAND

Gemmological Society of Finland
P.O. Box 6287
Helsinki, Finland

## FRANCE

French Diamond Association
7 Rue de Chatesudun
Paris 75009, France
Claude Varnier

Service Public Du Controle
2, Place de la Bourse
Paris 75002, France
Mr. Poirot

Syndicat des Maitres Artisans bijoutiers - joailliers
3, Rue Sainte - Elisabeth
75003 Paris, France

## GERMANY

Deutsch Gemmologische Gesellschaft EV
(German Gemmological Society)
Prof. - Schlossmacher - Str. 1
Postfach 122260
6580 Idar - Oberstein 2, West Germany

Diamant - und Edelsteinborse, Ida - Oberstein E.V.
Mainzer Str. 34
D-6580 Idar - Oberstein, West Germany

## HONG KONG

The Gemmological Association of Hong Kong
TST P.O. Box 97711
Kowloon, Hong Kong

Hong Kong Gemmologists' Assoc.
P.O. Box 74170
Kowloon Central Post Office, Hong Kong

## INDIA

The All India Jewellers Assoc.
19 Connaught Place
New Delhi, India

Andhra Pradesh Gold, Silver, Jewellery and Diamond Merchants
Association
Secunderabad, India

Bangiya Swarna Silpi Samitee
162 Bipin Behari Ganguli Street
Calcutta 12, India

Bombay Jewellers Association
308 Sheikh Memom Street
Bombay 400 002

The Cultured & Natural Pearl Association
1st Agiary Lane, Dhanji Street
Bombay 400 003, India

Gem & Jewellery Information Centre of India
A-95, Jana Colony
Journal House
Jaipur 302 004

Gujarat State Gold Dealers and Jewellers Association
2339-2, Manek Chowk
Ahmedabad, India

Jewellers' Association
Nagarthpet
Bangalore 560 002, India

Tamil Nadu Jewellers Federation (also the Madras Jwlers. & Dia.
Merch. Assoc.)
11/12 Car St., Netaji Subhaschandra Road
Madras 600 001

### INDONESIA

L.G. Tampubolon
Indonesian Gemstone & Jewellery Assoc.
J1. Teuku Umar 53
Jakarta 10310, Indonesia

# ISRAEL

Gemmological Association of Israel
1 Jabotinsky St.
Ramat-Gan, 5250, Israel

Israel Precious Stones Exchange
Maccabi Building, 1 Jabotinsky Street
Ramat-Gan 52520, Israel
Yehuda Kassif

# ITALY

CIBJO
Lungo Tevere Osali Anguillarh 9
Roma 00153, Italy
Dr. Amirante

Instituto Gemmologico Italiane
Piazzale Gambrare, 7/8
20146 Milano, Italy

# JAPAN

CIBJO of Japan
Chuo-Jiho Bldg. 3.1-3 Shintomi
2 Chome, Chuo-ku, Tokyo, Japan

Gemmoligical Association of All Japan
Tokyo Biho Kaikan
24 Akashi-chu, Chuo-ku, Tokyo 104 Japan

# KENYA

Kenya Gemstone Dealers Assoc.
P.O. Box 47928
Nairobi, Kenya
Dr. N.R. Barot

## MALAYSIA

Malaysian Institute of Gemmological Sciences
Lot 3, 76-3, 78 3$^{rd}$ Floor
Wisma Stephens
Jalan Caja Chulma, Kuala Lumpur

## NETHERLANDS

CIBJO-International Confederation of Jewellery, Silverware,
Diamonds, Pearls and Stones
Van de Spiegelstratte #3, P.O. Box 29818
The Hague, Netherlands 2502LV
Dr. Bernard W. Buenk, President

## PAKISTAN

All Pakistan Gem Merch. & Jwlrs. Association
1$^{st}$ Floor, Gems & Jewellery Trade Centre
Blenken Street
Saddar Karachi-3, Pakistan

## SINGAPORE

Singapore Gemologist Society
3, Lengkok Marak
Singapore-1024

## SOUTH AFRICA

Gem'l Assoc. of South Africa
P.O. Box 4216
Johannesburg 2000, South Africa
A.   Thomas

## SRI LANKA

Gemmologists Association of Sri Lanka
Professional Centre, 275-76
Baudhaloka Mawatha
Colombo-7, Sri Lanka

## SWEDEN

Swedish Association of Gemmologists
Birger Jarlsgatan 88
S-114 20 Stockholm, Sweden
Ake Gewers

Swedish Geological Society
c/o SGU, Box 670
S-751 28 Uppsala, Sweden

## SWITZERLAND

The Swiss Society of Gemmology
Kanagase 6,
Biel, Switzerland

Scheweizerische
Gemmologische, Gesellschaft
St. Gallen, Switzerland

Swiss Gem Trade Association
Nuschelerstr. 44
8001 Zurich, Switzerland
Dr. Christopher Kerez

## THAILAND

Asian Institute of Gemmological Sciences
987 Silom Road
Rama Jewellery Building
4th Floor, Bangkok 5

Thai Gems and Jewelry Assoc.
33/85 Surawongse Road, 17<sup>th</sup> Floor
Bangkok 10500, Thailand
            and at
942/152 Charn Issara Tower, 15<sup>th</sup> Floor
Rama 4 Road, Bangkok 10500, Thailand

## ZAMBIA

Zambia Gemstone & Precious Metal Association
P.O. Box 31099, Room 17
Luangwa House
Cairo Road, Lusaka, Zambia

## ZIMBABWE

Gem Education Centre of Zimbabwe
Founders House
15 Gordon Avenue
Harare, Zimbabwe 707580
Lesley Faye Marsh, F.G.A.

# APPENDIX F

## INTERNATIONAL DIRECTORY OF GEMOLOGICAL LABORATORIES

### AUSTRALIA

ACT Institute of T.A.F.E.
Gemmology Dept.
P.O. Box 273, Civic Square,
ACT, 2608 Australia
Tel. 451798

Australian Gemmologist
P.O. Box 35
South Yarra, Victoria 3141, Australia

Gemmological Association of Australia
Queensland Div.
20 Rosslyn St.
East Brisbane, Queensland, Australia 4169
Tel. (07) 3915

S. Australia Div., Box 191
Adelaide, S. Australia 5001
Western Australia Div., P.O. Box 355
Nedlands, West Australia

### AUSTRIA

Austrian Gemmological Research Institute
Salesianergasse, 1
A-1030 Vienna, Austria
Tel. (222) 71168, Ext. 318 or 260

### BELGIUM

European Gemmological Laboratory
Rjifstraat, 3
2018 Anrtwerp, Belgium
Tel. 233 82 94

Hoge Raad voor Diamant
Hoveniersstraat, 22
B-2018 Antwerp, Belgium

## CANADA

Brodman Gemmological Lab., Inc.
1255 Phillips Square #1105
Montreal, Quebec, Canada H3B 3G1
Tel. (514) 866-4081

De Goutiere Jewellers, Ltd.
2542 Estevan Avenue
Victoria, British Columbia, Canada V8R 2S7
Tel. (604) 592-3224
A.   De Goutiere, (CGA)

Ernest Penne Inc.
53 Queen Street
St. Catherines, Ontario, Canada L2R 5GB
Tel. (416)  688-0579
Ernest Penner (CGA)

Gem Service Lab
Harold Weinstein Ltd.
55 Queen St., E. 1301
Toronto, Ontario, Canada  M5C 1R6
Tel. 366-6518

The Gold Shop
345 Quellette Avenue
Windsor, Ontario Canada  N9A 4J1
Tel. (519)  254-5166
Ian M. Henderson (CGA)

Kinnear d'Esterre Jeweller
168 Princess Street
Kingston, Ontario Canada  K7L 1B1
Tel. (613)  546-2261
Erling Alstrup (CGA)

Nash Jewellers
182 Dundas Street
London, Ontario Canada N6A 1G7
Tel. (519) 672-7780
John C. Nash (CGA)

## ENGLAND

British Museum (Natural History)
Department of Mineralogy
Cromwell Road
London SW7 5BD, England
Tel. (01) 938-9123

The Gem Testing Laboratory
27 Greville Street
Saffron Hill Entrance
London E1N8SU, England

Huddlestone Gemmological Consultants Ltd.
100 Hatton Garden, Suite 221
London ECIN 8NX, England
Tel. 01-404-5004
Sunderland Polytechnic Gemmological Laboratory
Dept. of Applied Geology,
Benedict Bldg., St. George's Way
Stockton Road
Sunderland, SR2 7BW, England
Tel. (091) 567-9316

## FRANCE

European Gemological Laboratory
9, Rue Buffault
75009 Paris, France
Tel. (1) 40-16-16-35

Laboratoire Public De Controle des Pierres Preciuses de la Chambre De Commerce (C.C.I.P.)
2, Place De La Bourse
75002 Paris, France
Tel. 40268312

## GERMANY

Deutsches Diamant Institut
Poststrasse I
Postfach 470
D-7530 Pforzheim, Germany
Tel. 07231/32211

Deustsches Edelstein
Testinstitut (only gemstones)
Mainzerstrasse 34
D-6850 Idar-Oberstein, Germany

Deustsche Gemmologische Gesellaschaft EV
Prof.-Schlossmacher-Strasse 1
D6580 Idar-Oberstein 2, Germany
Tel. 6781/4-30-11

German Foundation of Gemstone Research (DSEF)
Prof.-Schlossmacher-Str. 1
D-6850 Idar Oberstein, Germany
Tel. 6781/4-30-13

## HONG KONG

Yang Mulia Gem Technological Consultancy and Laboratories
1103, Blissful Bldg.
247 Des Voeux Road Central
Hong Kong
Tel. 5-8152705

*International Gemological Laboratories*

# INDIA

Gem Identification Laboratory
372 Gopal Ji Ka Rasta
Jaipur 302003, India
Tel. 47528

Gemological Institute of India
29 Gurukul Chambers
187 Mumbadevi Rd.
Bombay 400 002, India

Gem Testing Laboratory
Rajasthan Chamber
Mirza Ismail Rd.
Jaipur, India

# ISRAEL

Gemological Institute for Precious Stones
52 Bazalel St., 1$^{st}$ Floor
Ramat Gan 52521, Israel

National Gemological Institute of Israel
52 Bazalel St.
Ramat Gan 52521, Israel
Tel. 751-7102

# ITALY

Analisi Consulenze Gemmologiche
Via Totrino, 5
15048 Valenza (Alessandria) Italy
Tel. 0131-953161

Centro Analisi Gemmologiche
Viale Vicenza 4/D
15048 Valenze, Italy

Cisgem-External Service for Precious Stones/Chamber of Commerce of Milan
Via Brisa/Via Ansperto, 5
20123 Milano, Italy
Tel. 02/85155499

Instituto Analisi Gemmologiche
Via Sassi, 44
15048 Valenza, Italy
Tel. 0131-946586

Instituto Gemmologico Italiano
Viale Gramsci, 228
20099 Sesto San Giovanni
Milano, Italy
Tel. (02) 2409354
also at
Via Appia Nuova, 52
00183 Roma, Italy
Tel. (06) 7575685

Laboratorio Scientifico
Professionale di Controllo di
Diamanti, Pietre Preziose e
Perle della CONFEDORAFI
Via Ugo Foscolo 4
1-20121 Milano, Italy

### HOLLAND

Nederlands Edelsteen Laboratorium (only gemstones)
Hooglandse Kergracht 17
2312 HS Leiden, Nederland
Tel. (31) 071-143844

Stichting Nederlands Diamant Institut (only diamonds)
Van de Spiegelstraat 3
Postbus 29818
NL-2502LV's-Gravenhage, Nederland
Tel. 070-469607

*International Gemological Laboratories*

# JAPAN

Central Gem Lab
Taiyo Bldg. 15017, 5 Chome,
Ueno, Taito-Ku
Tokyo, 110, Japan
Tel. 03-836-3131

CIBJO Institute of Japan (only diamonds)
Tokyo-Bihokaikan 1-24, Akashi-Cho
Chuo-Ku, Tokyo, Japan
Tel. 03-543-3821

# KENYA

Mr. P. Duogan
P.O. Box 14173
Nairobi, Kenya
Ruby Center of Kenya Ltd.
Fedha Towers, Second Floor
Muindi Mbingu Street
Nairobi, Kenya (East Africa)
Tel. 335261, 334299

# KOREA

Mi-Jo Gem Study Institute
244-39, Huam-dong Youngsan-ku
Seoul, Korea  140-190
Tel. 754-5075, 0642

# REPUBLIC OF SOUTH AFRICA

European Gemological Laboratory
Paulshop Bldg.
Corner Plein & Twist Streets
Johannesburg, South Africa
Tel. 29-9647

Gem Education Center
508 Medical Arts Bldg.
220 Jeppe Street
Johannesburg, 2000, South Africa
Tel. 337-3457, 3458

Independent Coloured Stones Lab
5 Hengilcon Avenue
Blairgourie, Randburg Transvaal,
Rep. Of South Africa 2194
Tel. (011) 787-3326

## SINGAPORE

International Gemological Lab, (S) Pte. Ltd.
402 Orchard Road
#03-07, Delfi Orchard
Singapore 0923
Tel. 732-7272 / 732-3636

## SPAIN

Instituto Gemologico Espanol
Victor Hugo, 1, 3e
Madrid-4, Spain

Laboratorio Oficial de la Association Espanola de Gemologia AEG
Pseo. De Gracia 64 entr. 2a
Barcelona-7, Spain
Tel. 2 15 43 12

## SRI LANKA

Gemological Association of Sri Lanka Professional Center
125/75 Bauddhalokka Mawatha
Colombo 7, Sri Lanka

Gemmology Laboratory/Department of Mining & Minerals
Engineering
University of Moratuwa
Katubedde, Sri Lanka
Tel. Colombo 505353

Petrological Laboratory
Geological Survey Department
48, Sri Jinaratana Rd.
Colombo 2, Sri Lanka
Tel. 29014/15

State Gem Corporation
No. 92/4A, Templars Road
Mount Lavinia, Sri Lanka

## SWEDEN

Swedish Institute for Gem Testing
P.O. Box 3021
S-12703 Stockholm, Sweden

Rolf Krieger
Kungsgatan 32 VI
S 1111 35 Stockholm, Sweden
Tel. 8/ 10-13-65

## SWITZERLAND

Gemgrading
4,Rue Albert-Gos
1206 Geneva, Switzerland
Tel. (022) 46-60-61

Gemmological Lab Gubelin
Denkmalstrasse, 2
Ch-6006 Luzern, Switzerland

Gemmologie Laboratoire Service
Rue de Bourg, 3
1003 Lausanne, Switzerland
Tel. (021) 20-49-77

Schweizerische Stiftung Fur Edelstein-Forschung (SSEF)
Lowentrasse 17,
CH-8001 Zurich, Switzerland
Tel. 01/211 24 71

## THAILAND

Asian Institute of Gemmological Science
987 Silom Rd.
Rama Jewellery Bldg., 4$^{th}$ Floor
Bangkok 10500, Thailand
Tel. 233-8388/9, 235-1254/5

## ZIMBABWE

Gem Education Centre of Zimbabwe
Founders House 15 Gordon Avenue
Harare, Zimbabwe 707580

# APPENDIX G

## DIAMOND PRICE SOURCES

*Precious Stones Market Monitor.* Gemological Appraisal Association, 666 Washington Road, Pittsburgh, Pennsylvania 15228.

*The Diamond Registry.* 30 West 47th Street, New York, New York 10036.

*Diamond Insight.* Tyron Mercantile Inc., 50 East 66th Street, 2A, New York, New York 10021.

*The Guide.* Gemworld International, Inc., 5 South Wabash, Chicago, Illinois 60602.

*Michelsen Gemstone Index.* Gem Spectrum, 1401 South Dixie Highway East, #5, Pompano Beach, Florida 33060.

*Rapaports Diamond Reports.* 15 West 47th Street, New York, NY.

# APPENDIX H

## TOOLS & EQUIPMENTS SUPPLIERS

Albert Froidevaux & Sons/USA
Albert Froidevaux et Fils S.A., Switzerland
11449 Randall Dr.
Lenexa, KS 66215
913-338-3131                    Fax. 913-338-3144

B. Jadow & Sons, Inc.
Vigor/Jemeter (Vigor tools and equipment available from distributors)
53 W. 23$^{rd}$ St.
New York, NY 10010
212-807-3800                    Fax. 212-645-8637

Berco Watch & Jewelers Supply
29 East Madison
Chicago, IL 60602
312-782-1050                    Fax. 312-982-4441

Borel & Frei
712 S. Olive Street
Los Angeles, CA 90014
213-689-4630                    Fax: 213-488-0485

Bourget Bros
1636 11$^{th}$ St.
Santa Monica, CA 90404
213-450-6556

Carl Zeiss, Inc.
One Zeiss Drive
Thornwood, NY 10594
914-747-1800

Cas-Ker Co.
2121 Spring Grove Ave.
P.O. Box 14069
Cincinnati, OH 45214
513-241-7073                    Fax. 513-241-5848

*Tools & Equipments Suppliers*

Colmans-Borel
812 Huron Rd., Ste. 600
Cleveland, OH
216-771-2343          Fax. 216-771-7304

Columbia School of Gemology
8600 Fenton Street
Silver Spring, MD 20910
301-588-7770

The Contenti Co.
123 Stewart St.
Providence, RI 02903
800-343-3364          Fax. 401-421-4040

Dallas Jewelry Supply House
9979 Monroe Dr.
Dallas, TX 75220
214-351-2263          Fax. 800-346-5397

S. Fargotstein & Son
P.O. Box 111049
2505 Poplar Ave.
Memphis, TN
901-452-8475          Fax. 901-452-2600

Findco, Inc.
5444 Westheimer Rd., Ste. 635
Houston, TX 77056
713-995-8380

Gemlab, Inc.
P.O. Box 6333
Clearwater, FL 34618
813-447-1667          Fax. 813-442-1221

Gemmological Instruments, Ltd.
St. Dunstan's House
Carey Lane
London EC2V 8AB England
01-726-4374          Fax. 01-726-4837

Gemological Products Corporation
2834 Colorado Blvd., #14
Santa Monica, CA 90404
213-398-2567

Gemstone Press
P.O. Box 276
South Woodstock, VT 05071
802-457-4000/800-962-4544          Fax. 802-457-4004

GIA Gem Instruments
Gemological Institute of America
P.O. Box 2110
1660 Stewart St.
Santa Monica, CA 90406
213-829-2991                    Fax. 213-828-0247
          and
580 Fifth Avenue
New York, NY 10036
212-221-5858

Goldberg & Co., Inc.
725 Sansom St.
Philadelphia, PA 19106
215-922-0664

Hammel, Riglander & Co.
750 Washington Avenue
Carlstadt, NJ 07072
201-935-0100

Hanneman Gemological Instruments
P.O. Box 2453
Castro Valley, CA 94546
414-847-4391

Jewelers Equip. & Tools Corp.
5 North Wabash St., #818
Chicago, IL 60602
312-263-8221

I Kassoy, Inc.
28 W. 47th St.
New York, NY  10036
212-719-2290                     Fax. 212-575-1883

Sy Kessler Sales, Inc.
2263-C Valdina St.
Dallas, TX  75207
214-630-2563                     Fax, 214-632-2568

Leeds Precision Instruments
801 Boone Ave. N.
Minneapolis, MN  55427
612-546-8575                     Fax. 612-546-4369

J.F. McCaughin Co.
2628 N. River Ave.
Rosemead, CA  91770
818-573-5781, 213-623-6210
Fax. 818-307-6912

Nikon Inc. Instrument Division
623-T Stewart Avenue
Garden City, NY  11530
516-222-0200

Otto Frei-Jules Borel Co.
P.O. Box 796
126 2nd St.
Oakland, CA  94604
415-832-0355

Page & Wilson, Ltd.
330 W. Pender St.
Vancouver, BC
Canada, V6B 3K2
604-685-8257

Nebula
P.O. Box 3356
Redwood City, CA 94064
415-369-5966

Norman Press, Inc.
18345 Ventura Blvd., Ste. 305
Tarzana, CA 91356
818-343-4655

Raytech Industries
P.O. Box 6
Stafford Springs, CT 06076
203-684-4273

Roseco, Inc.
8111 LBJ, Ste. 840
Dallas, TX 75271
214-437-9129

Rosenthal Jewelers Supply Corp.
138 N.E. 1$^{st}$ Ave.
Miami, FL 31132
305-371-5661                    Fax. 305-577-8275

Rubin & Son Diamond & Jewelry Supplies/USA
96 Spring St.
New York, NY 10012
212-966-6300                    Fax. 212-966-6354

Sarasota Instruments, Inc.
Jemeter, 1960 Main St.
Sarasota, FL 34236
813-366-4646

Spectronics Corporation
956-T Brush Hollow Road
Westbury, NY 11590
516-333-4840

Swest, Inc.
P.O. Box 540938, 10803 Composite Dr.
Dallas, TX 75354
214-350-4011                    Fax. 214-357-9664

Transcontinental Tool Co.
21 Dundas Sq. #605
Toronto, ON, Canada M5B 1B7
416-363-7251

Tulper & Co.
2223 E. Colfax St.
Denver, CO 80206
303-399-9291

Vibrograf USA Corp.
504 Cherry Ln.
Floral Park, NY 11001
516-437-8700

# BIBLIOGRAPHY

Eric Bruton. *Legendary Gems or Gems That Made History*. PA: Chilton Book Co., 1986

Fred Cuellar . *How To Buy A Diamond*. IL: Casablanca Press, 1998

Jay Feder. *The Practical Guide To Buying Diamonds*. CO: Four C's Press, 1986

David Marcum. *Guide To Fine Gems and Jewelry*. Il: Dow Jones-Irwin, 1986

Joseph Mirsky. *Consumer Guide To Diamonds*. NJ: 1995

Renee Newman. *Diamond Ring Guide*. LA: International Jewelry Pub., 1998

Readers Digest. *Strange Stories, Amazing Facts*. 1977

Simon & Schuster's *Guide To Gems & Precious Stones*. NY: Fireside Book, 1986

Fred Ward. *Diamonds*. MD: Gem Book Publishers, 1998

Mab Wilson. *Gems*. NY: The Viking Press, 1967

## About the Author

B.J. Tadena's perseverance is paying off. He has achieved so much of his objectives in life and in his chosen field in the diamond industry. His relentless pursuit of his place in the trade exposed him to numerous experiences which never clouded his optimism and determination.

B.J. Tadena acquired his skill in Europe where he first started as rough stones sorter to polished stones sorter. He went on to work through the whole process of diamond cutting and brillianteering. He was able to know them well enough that he was able to design specific machinery and equipments to suit the needs of the company.

Multiligual in his own right (conversant in four languages), B.J. Tadena has travelled extensively in Europe and now travels to Africa visiting diamond factories and mines. A master diamond cutter, dealer and broker, B.J. Tadena is also the Chairman and CEO of Rough Stones Co., Inc., a New York-based corporation engaged in diamond explorations and mining. He was the publisher of the MCNNews Magazine and the author of the article "This Rock Is Hard To Crack, The Art of Diamond Cutting".

Currently, B.J. Tadena is conducting seminars and workshops focused primarily on diamond cutting and other intricacies of the trade. He had conducted similar seminars before in San Francisco attended by a number of gemologists, lapidary groups and jewelers. His craft is his passion and he continues to design machines and equipments in relation to his craft.